MAKE THEM WORK (FOR YOU)

How To Motivate Successful Teams

100 motivational tips based on real cases

Practical Handbook For Leaders

BORIS GRAMCHEV

Copyright © 2019 by Boris Gramchev.

All Rights Reserved.

No part of this publication may be reproduced, distributed, or transmitted in any form or by any means, including photocopying, recording, or other electronic or mechanical methods, or by any information storage and retrieval system without the prior written permission of the author/publisher, except in the case of brief quotations embodied in critical reviews and certain other non-commercial uses permitted by copyright law. For permission requests, write to the author at gramchev@marimex-bg.com

All cases, tips and solutions in this book are meant to assist you in establishing motivational culture in your organization and increasing the motivation of your employees, subordinates, and/or team members. They do not guarantee any results. The advices and strategies contained herein may not be suitable for your situation. Any tips undertaken are carried out at your own risk. No responsibility is taken by the author and/or the publisher for any consequences resulting from anything you do as a result of reading this book. You are advised to consult with a professional where appropriate.

Make Them Work (For You) is the first book of
Team Functioning Books Series, supported by:

Institute of Team Functioning

Odessos Consulting Group

"We should all look more closely at our inner self so as to see ourselves as people who have a role to play in a larger story, and not just seek personal advancement."

Helen Young Hayes
Founder & CEO at Activate Workforce Solutions PBC.

"It's the job of a manager not to light the fire of motivation, but to create an environment to let each person's personal spark of motivation blaze."

Frederick Herzberg
Founder of the *Two factor theory of motivation*

CONTENTS

Introduction	9
Historical Overview of Motivation Theory	11
Three Important Conditions	15
Motivational Culture	18
1. Payment & Benefits	22
2. Team Relations	26
2.1 Teamwork and Collaboration	27
2.2 Recognition and Respect from Colleagues	31
2.3 Internal Competition	34
2.4 Colleagues' Personalities	37
3. Organization	42
3.1 Promotion Opportunities	43
3.2 Job Security	47
3.3 Trainings and Team-buildings	51
3.4 Working Conditions	56
3.5 Workload	59
3.6 Instructions and Targets	64
3.7 Decision-Making Rights	70
3.8 Work Time Flexibility	76
4. Superiors	83
4.1 Relationship with Management	85

4.2 Trust between Managers and Subordinates	90
5. Personal Life Factors	96
5.1 Recognition from Friends and Family	98
5.2 Social Status	99
5.3 Personal Satisfaction	103
Conclusion	107
About The Author	110
Bibliography	111

INTRODUCTION

Motivation is what propels life. It plays a major role in nearly everything we do. Without motivation, we would simply not care about means, outcomes, accomplishment, education, success, failure, and so on. Managers often confuse the idea of *satisfied* employees with the one of *motivated* employees. Although they may be related, motivation actually describes the level of desire employees feel to perform, regardless of their levels of satisfaction and happiness.

By default, each manager should be keenly aware of differences in their subordinates' levels of motivation. Motivated employees who have a strong sense of commitment manifest proactive involvement in the work process and proclaim their readiness to be of service. These employees arrive early at the workplace, complete the assigned tasks on time, and actively participate in both external and internal professional activities. Contrariwise, employees who do not show a strong commitment are less eager to initiate or develop their personal career opportunities. It becomes the responsibility of the manager, then, to deal with this lack of motivation, especially when it impacts job performance.

Whether internal or external, the reasons for demotivation are various. Maybe some basic needs are unmet, or maybe employees are not sure what you expect from them. Circumstances and situations that deprive people from motivation may differ, but one fact is certain - helping your employees build greater understanding of the factors that can boost both their professional and personal satisfaction is a must for modern management. In addition, successful leadership relies on the leader having four main abilities: *clarifying demands, imposing responsibilities, showing commitment,* and *stating expected results.* These are the points, upon which are formed the so-called *golden MBO-questions,* which all managers should explicate to their employees. They are also known as the *1-million-dollar-questions* (according to a research in the last decade, which found that corporations which have clarified these 4 points with all of their employees increase their revenue by USD 1 million per annum):

How managers should… / *Questions to discuss with the employees*

…clarify demands: *"What do we demand from you?"*

…impose responsibilities: *"For what shall we hold you responsible?"*

…show commitment: *"What do you need in order to fulfill your obligations?"*

…state expected results: *"What result shall we expect from you?"*

Therefore, working on synchronizing employees' expectations and needs with those of the company may increase their motivation and help you by ensuring they work for you more effectively and efficiently. Let's see how this can be done in practice!

HISTORICAL OVERVIEW OF MOTIVATION THEORY

The studies of motivation over the past decades have proposed various motivation theories, but perhaps the most fundamental and well known is Abraham Maslow's (1943) *Hierarchy of Needs*. In addition to the pyramidal construct of needs, the revolutionary premise of Maslow's theory is that higher-level needs become activated only when lower-level needs are satisfied. For example, if an employee comes to work not having slept over the last night, fatigue will be the prime motivator and he may be unable to attend to higher-level needs, such as achievement or creativity. Likewise, if a manager feels diminished job security at work, it will be more difficult for him to focus on team goals. In essence, higher-level needs cannot be pursued or even felt, until lower-level needs are largely satisfied. This understanding can help managers to focus on considering if an employee's basic needs are met in order for that individual to be able to strive for higher-level goals, whether self or company related.

Another landmark research on motivation is Frederick Herzberg's (1959) *Two Factor theory*. It was derived from Maslow's Hierarchy of Needs, but does not have any such hierarchical arrangement. The model examines two distinct categories that relate to motivation issues. The positive aspects of an employee's job are *satisfiers,* while the negative aspects are *dissatisfiers*. Satisfiers, include the employee's degree of accountability, opportunities for advancement and growth, the sense of achievement and the nature of the work itself. Dissatisfiers, on the other hand, include such factors as payment, job security, working conditions, organizational policies, status, and the relationship with the superiors. Herzberg believes that eliminating dissatisfiers will rarely improve an employee's performance. It only can reduce the frustrations and irritations among the employees. The reason for this is that satisfaction and dissatisfaction are not polar opposites. For example, managing employees' dissatisfaction by offering them higher payment does not necessarily mean the employees will then be satisfied. They will just no longer be dissatisfied. In order to motivate them to higher levels of performance, managers need to work on the satisfiers making changes in the structure and nature of the work itself.

In 1964 another significant study was published that continues the line of development of motivation science. It is Victor Vroom's (1964) *Expectancy Theory*, focused on the rational and conscious aspects of employee motivation and the factors related with levels of low and high productivity. According to this theory, an individual is going to select his behavior based on the outcomes that he expects as a result of that behavior. For example, imagine your employees arriving at the office in the morning. At the beginning of the working day they have two basic alternatives – they can decide to work really hard all day long, reaching beyond what is expected of them and helping the company grow. Or, conversely, they can meet their requirements, performing just enough to get by and going no further. Which way, do you think, are they going to choose? Vroom proves they will tend to select the way that makes the most sense for them as employees, based on the rewards and compensation available. If the rewards for working really hard and working just hard enough to get by are nearly the same, most of your employees will tend to perform as little as possible. After all, what will be their motivation to work harder? People will be motivated to strive for their best only when you offer them rewards that are commensurable with their efforts.

Vroom uses three beliefs as variables to account for his theory. These are *expectancy, instrumentality,* and *valence. Expectancy* refers to the belief that employees have different expectations and confidence in their capabilities which influence the achievement of their performance goals. Management has to find out what resources, support, or training they need. *Instrumentality* is the arrangement that employees will receive a reward if the performance goals are met. Management then has to ensure that they will actually get what they have been promised. As regards *valence*, it is the value employees place on the rewards of their outcome. Management, therefore, needs to discover what they value by observing how emotional they become towards the rewards. Vroom suggests that employees' perceptions of Expectancy, Instrumentality, and Valence interact psychologically to create a motivational force which explains how much employees will tend to act in ways that avoid suffering or bring pleasure. Hence, as the *motivational force* is the multiplication of the expectancy by the instrumentality it is then through valence that any belief having a value of zero or the employee's feeling that *it is not going to happen*, will result in a *zero* motivational force.

Though the *Expectancy Theory* of motivation has been the subject of many critics it has prevailed and been accepted by business societies as a reasonable and rational model that explains employees' individual decision-making. It's without question that through including a predictive value, *Expectancy theory* may empower managers to increase the probability of an employee acting out the desired behavior or outcome. However, attempts to implement the theory in an organizational context won't be an easy task!

I personally believe that despite their age, the models of Herzberg and Vroom provide excellent guidelines for motivating a modern team. They are focused on improvements in the psychological contract between employers and their employees with regards to common expectations of inputs and outcomes. Moreover, both models are applicable to different types of organizations and largely support management's position. Personally, having used the ideas in these theories many times in the course of my professional practice, this book is, as a result, ideologically synchronized with them. Of course, there are other motivation theories, but for now we need to remain focused on how to practically establish a motivational culture in your organization and most of all – what is it *in praxis?*

THREE IMPORTANT CONDITIONS

From a psychological perspective, employee motivation is the relative strength of identification of the employees with a particular work process or outcome. It determines their involvement in these processes and outcomes and is characterized by acceptance of the goals, belief in the value of the consequences, desire to exert oneself, and willingness to remain committed until goals are accomplished.

To a large extent, the success of a company depends on the degree to which its employees can integrate the goals of their teams into their own structure of values and needs. This unique sense of belonging is the essence of organizational commitment. It goes along with personal motivation and represents the anticipation that employees will achieve satisfaction from being a part of the company. Such interdependence based on achieving common goals and objectives leads to relationships of respect and trust. They reinforce teamwork and increase productivity. The challenge for managers, therefore, is to help employees develop feelings of cohesion and solidarity, as well as a strong sense of personal ownership and accountability within the context of a company. In order to achieve this, management must focus their efforts on establishing three essential conditions: *relevance, influence,* and *community*.

Relevance.

In our dynamic world employees tend to expect that their talents and skills are being used appropriately and the effort and time they dedicate to important tasks and missions help the company in achieving its strategic goals. Very often employees feel they are overburdened with pointless, time-consuming work, much of which is due to micromanagement or lack of managerial competence. Irrelevant tasks diminish the sense of purpose and meaning that is so crucial to commitment. They encourage resistance, justify negative behavior, and finally, destroy motivation.

Influence.

Employees need to know that their actions and behaviors make a difference. It is in our human nature to strive for acknowledgement that what we are doing matters. Influence refers to our personal feelings of importance. A salesperson, for example, may feel like he makes a difference in the lives of his clients and may derive a great deal of personal satisfaction from the work he does every day. But in addition, he also needs feedback that the work he performs has a positive influence on what happens in the company.

Community.

Relevance cannot become a collective experience and the sense of influence and personal contribution cannot become a shared organizational feature, until a certain level of mutual cooperation and interdependence is reached. Each organization needs a policy, guaranteeing compliance and fostering of norms of interdependence and collegiality. And this is where building a motivational culture starts. By fostering harmony, mutual respect and solidarity, such policy creates a sense of community and an environment of shared responsibility for everyone's well-being. Community is based on the sense of unity and a perception of belonging. It refers to the constructive belief that people can depend on one another.

Based on the above motivational paradigm the tips and solutions in this book are meant to support the efforts of management in establishing a motivational culture with the desired level of *relevance, influence,* and *community* in their organizations.

MOTIVATIONAL CULTURE

Have you ever asked yourself why some employees show initiative and a strong desire to achieve company goals while others do not? Why certain incentives can stimulate high performance in some employees and not others? People's behavior is determined by two kinds of factors that distinguish what they *can do* from what they *want to do*. The first refers to the level of competence, while the second is related to attitude. And where attitude is involved, it has to do with one's level of motivation. Commitment and devotion to work, therefore, has a direct relation to the level of motivation people exhibit. However, our understanding of motivation should not result only from the expectation that employees' efforts will lead to anticipated outcomes. Our understanding of motivation should be a multifunctional amalgam of theoretical knowledge, practical experience and gut feelings that empower us to separate all motivational factors and scrutinize them independently, though they may seem strongly interdependent. Understanding them means knowing how to empower a culture of motivation, which can be critical to sustaining or improving the daily work of the company and its overall success.

Motivational culture encompasses values, principles and behaviors that contribute to establishing a unique psychological and social environment within an organization, oriented towards commitment and productivity. It is a product of a set of factors that cause the employees to act in a certain way and pursue their work tasks and goals. These factors play a role of inner or social stimulus for action, and thus motivation has two main origins – extrinsic and intrinsic.

The *extrinsic motivational factors* are external and cause the employees to act toward fulfillment of their individual or team tasks and objectives. Usually, these are in the form of punishments or rewards. The former forces employees to act in order to avoid a punishment, while the latter stimulates them to act in order to receive a reward. The *intrinsic factors of motivation*, on the other hand, are forces that come from within an employee. People are intrinsically motivated to work when the work itself motivates them. In most cases, they find the work satisfying, fulfilling or enjoyable. Thus, the work itself provides the motivation. Intrinsic factors are often more effective than the extrinsic ones, because they derive from the inner readiness of the employees rather than being imposed on them. However, the intrinsic motivational factors are harder to facilitate. To support them, managers may specifically design the job to empower the employees to make decisions on their own. Usually, people are more motivated in their work, if they have more control and autonomy. Providing them with the ability to be creative and innovative will also improve their job satisfaction. Therefore, establishing a culture that values exploration and encourages learning will enrich the work environment and will facilitate the intrinsic motivational factors.

In addition to building a motivational culture, there is another matter managers must enact if they want to deepen employee commitment and bolster motivation. Specifically, this factor has to do with their own motivation. John Adair (2006) has described fifty-five rules of motivation, but the first and golden one is that the leader will never inspire the others, unless he is inspired himself. Indeed, only the motivated can be found to be motivating. Following on Fleischman's twenty years research on leadership motives, the *personal orientation motive* appears to be the strongest one. Further, in spite of the leader's limited power and ability to motivate the others, he or she could do a great job by creating an environment, which they will find personally motivating. Motivation, according to Hofstede (2001), is a force that constructs and explains people's behaviors and within these behaviors it is linked to organizational culture. In such a context, motivational culture is and should be perceived as part of the organizational culture. Economic development also strongly supports motivation, but there are other factors, and again mostly cultural, which predispose motivational behavior - for instance, the exposure to a parental role model of the organizational nature.

When we study employee motivation in a global aspect, it is also important to consider to what extent the theoretical assumptions conform to different populations. The way how cultural factors are connected to the basic motivational process is manifested by the perception of the goals. People from individualistic cultures are more inclined to focus on the performance of goals, than to master goals. The goals may reveal a different relation across different groups. The relations between the goals also differ due to cultural or ethnic reasons. However, when we analyze employee motivation in terms of team functioning, we need to explore the direct links between motivation and organizational culture and their various contributions to each other, rather than to stick to that motivation, which is a product of the goals' perception. For this reason, we need to combine three main levels of analysis, based on intrapsychological processes, interpersonal relationships, and organizational and interteam contexts. These make it possible to conceptualize employee motivation as a multidimensional construct internal to the individual, influenced by different situations, and reflected in the individual perceptions, decisions and behaviors. Motivational factors, therefore, are defined as individual factors that are essential for psychological satisfaction within a work environment and can be clustered into five domains: *payment and benefits, team relations, organization, superiors,* and *personal life factors*. Combining them envisages the connection between motivation and culture in one organization and shows how personal motivation understanding opens a wide door for approaches to culture and at the end reaches the point where culture affects the individual motives.

1. PAYMENT & BENEFITS

Human Resource Management has never been as significant as it is today. All companies compete to attract and motivate talents to meet their objectives. Today, employees are considered as one of the most important assets of every company, so they need to be effectively managed. The best tools companies use to attract, motivate and retain its people are the fair pay system and compensation management. Employers are ultimately responsible for ensuring that their pay systems are free from incorrect evaluation tendencies, based on practices such as, for example, gender bias, nepotism tolerance, or the halo effect.

Compensation can include monetary and non-monetary components. In practice, compensation often comprises an employee's base salary and additional benefits, such as health insurance, retirement plans and performance bonuses. The compensation packages offered by most business organizations to their employees seek to influence the recruitment and retention rate, and have a positive impact on employee satisfaction. Employee benefits are membership-based. Employees receive them regardless of their performance. However, the greatest impact on productivity is where performance is directly related to financial reward. For example, when a salesman knows that he will receive a bonus after achieving a certain sales quota this will most likely motivate him to raise his performance which will increase his productivity as well. For the same reasons, many employees are motivated to work hard for their companies and help them succeed, if they receive a decent share from the profit, mainly in the form of wage supplements, bonuses and other awards. Health insurance and retirement packages are also benefits that many employees desire from their employers. Companies that offer them have a much better chance of retaining workers than businesses that fail to do so.

Problem:

Many of the companies I visited as an external auditor had one cardinal problem in common. Specifically, the employees were demoralized by their payment and benefits. Many of them displayed a tendency of feeling underestimated and unfairly treated in financial terms. The subsequent lack of motivation impacted their team functioning, decreasing overall performance and poorer personal results. As managers usually realize how serious the problem is only when they are facing the first resignations, there is always a moment of urgency when it comes to dealing with the consequences of that issue.

Solution 1: *Increase the pay rate, starting from the best employees.*

If you want to keep your employees highly committed, maybe it is time to increase their payment, starting with the best ones. When you are considering your new pay system, take into account the industry benchmarks, but make sure you pay your star employees beyond what is considered the norm. Try to foresee the invaluable impact these persons bring to your company. There is a famous expression that you can never overpay good players - you can only overpay bad ones. In many cases, it is better to pay your best employees not merely because you *want* to keep them, but as if you desperately *need* to keep them. Other ways to retain the best employees is through regular promotions, which not only provide an employee with a higher base salary, but also the ability to take on more responsibility in the workplace.

Solution 2: *Offer flexible compensation packages.*

If you cannot afford increasing the payment rate of your employees, you may think about compensation packages. Attractive compensation packages can regain the motivation of the current employees and will play an important role in your company's ability to attract top talents as job candidates. However, you should keep in mind that the specific components of an attractive compensation package vary per employee. For example, a high base salary may attract a top job candidate that is 20-something and single, while a job candidate with a family may consider a flexible work schedule as extremely important. Having a diverse group of people in the workplace means that you may have to consider the various needs of those age groups when creating the employee benefits package. Allowing employees to pick and customize some of their benefits according to their needs may be more appealing than a "one-size-fits-all" approach. Benefit packages that offer choices and flexibility can drive participation, and can give employers a better return on investment. So you would have to carefully design your benefit package. It may include a cell phone to each employee, taking them to a training workshop or seminar, giving them a day or two off every month, and so on. While deciding on the benefits package, do consider the associated costs.

Solution 3: *Consider offering perks and rewards.*

Another method to increase the motivation of your employees is to offer them perks and rewards. They are not necessarily expensive. You can offer low-cost options, such as company-paid lunch breaks, cell phone service staff discounts, company car rental discount for personal use, an employee-of-the-month reward, dental or medical services, generous leave and holiday policy, and so on. You can use the *online perk platforms* to provide your employees with plenty of local, national or worldwide perks and discounts across health and spa, travel and hotels, sport and fitness, food and entertainment, shopping, finance, and much more. It would be great if you empower them to tailor their perks to their own personal needs and interests.

Creating a culture within your company that makes employees feel valued can also be a great tool for improving team functioning. When you ensure your *perks and rewards plan* suits both you and your employees, let them know about it and explain how much their *total compensation package* has been increased. Having them aware of the potential added value that their perks and rewards provide to their compensation package is always appreciated. So, don't underestimate the power of these tools to strengthen the working relationship with your employees and improve their performance.

2. TEAM RELATIONS

Strong employee relationships often lead to an increased degree of motivation among the team and result in higher productivity. Providing excellent atmosphere for healthy work relations would in turn benefit the whole organization. The workplace transforms into a much happier place, and the employees tend to focus more on work instead of unproductive activities. Everyone needs to charge their batteries from time to time and rely on their colleagues to avoid performance dips. Proper team relations act as a catalyst for an organization's success and help the members to remain productive and deliver good results everytime. According to the facts those employees who are motivated by strong team relations work better and at a much faster rate as compared to other motivational factors.

Indicators for strong team relations in terms of team functioning are: *strong teamwork and collaboration, recognition and respect from the colleagues, healthy internal competition,* and *properly selected personalities.*

2.1 TEAMWORK AND COLLABORATION

Teamwork and collaboration are vital factors for the success of any business organization. When the employees work effectively together and develop strong team relationships, they are more likely to enjoy their mutual work. Higher morale among the team means greater flow of information, increased personal performance, boosting of team productivity, and higher company profits. Most tasks do require some level of teamwork and collaboration. Teamwork depends on a complete recognition that the company goals and overall task accomplishment means putting aside personal views or desires. An important aspect of teamwork and collaboration includes the ability of the team members to conform to the strengths and weaknesses of their peers and coworkers. Everyone should be committed to listen to other points of view and respect different approaches for gaining the best results and completing the tasks set forth by company management. It's about the team winning and not the individual. This unselfishness has been, and will continue to be, a strong key component of team's success. Unfortunately, perfect teamwork and collaboration sounds like utopia and happens very rarely. In practice, there are always team members who find it difficult to work with each other. When the enthusiasm among the team is poor and inspiration is lacking, the team functioning suffers and leaders waste lots of time in vain trying to manage these teamwork issues.

Problem:

In the Chartering & Brokerage Department of a shipping company I noticed that the poor team productivity was mainly a result of bad teamwork, selfish individualism and lack of collaboration between the members. Shipbrokers and chartering agents, like many other brokers and agents in other fields, do not communicate that often between each other and are somehow reluctant to exchange important information or knowledge to protect their own personal contacts and interests. In that particular field, the losses from a single mistake or omission could be colossal. Though we cannot change this practice (and of course we don't need to), there are still some actions that can be carried out.

Solution:

If you have similar problems and need to establish or just improve the culture of collaboration within your organization, you should know something important: It's vital that your employees buy into it. It should become a natural part of team ethics, rather than something forced upon them by constant reminders and reinforcement. To build a collaborative culture among your team, there are a range of strategies that you may employ:

Tip 1: Focus on communication issues.

When the team has problems with teamwork and collaboration, your number one priority should be fostering open and clear communication channels between all team members, and especially between the team and their manager. The way employees communicate is essential to their teamwork and productivity. They need to feel comfortable and express their opinions confidently without fear of being ignored or belittled. The team manager should encourage everyone to share important information amongst the team, emphasizing the mutual goals and demonstrating the interdependent nature of the team jobs.

Tip 2: Empower creativity.

The team members should be encouraged to participate and contribute to all mutual work, and their new ideas should be valued. If their ideas are being heard, the employees are more likely to be

MAKE THEM WORK (FOR YOU)

motivated when they work alone or in collaboration with other colleagues. Certainly, only the best ideas can be used, but all of them have to be appreciated.

Tip 3: Make people who work remotely feel part of the project.

The boom in digital technologies encouraged many organizations to employ people who live in other parts of the world, as well as to allow their employees to work from home for some period of time. These team members are no less important than those you work with in the office. Organizations which have remote employees should invest in all of the necessary tools to guarantee that they feel connected. It's an obligation for management to integrate them into the team, keep them motivated and ensure they are familiar with every aspect of the project, in accordance with their job. What makes a unit great is that members don't allow distance to interfere with their ability to collaborate as a team. Therefore, the team manager should arrange regular communication between everyone in the team, whether it is by telephone, Skype, email, or other internet tools. If your organization does not have remote employees currently, but you think that you may consider having them for the future, just keep this tip in mind in order to ensure effective and productive workflow.

Tip 4: Include teamwork in performance appraisals.

Many managers tend to include easily measurable goals and targets in the performance appraisals, and then to forget or neglect important intangible factors such as how well a team member works within a team. A good way to improve the collaboration between the employees and bring them back to working together is to include teamwork in performance appraisals and make it an unambiguous part of performance measurement. Thus, the team will know their behavior and cohesion is being monitored and evaluated from time to time. It is important for them to understand that the team needs teamwork to reach their goals, and as a manager, you have to make sure they are living up to the cohesive standards you expect of them. By being straightforward and honest, and setting clear rules right from the beginning, your employees will be discouraged to complain they don't understand the responsibilities and requirements of their role. Sometimes, instead of rating each employee as an individual, appraise them on a group basis. This strategy will not only keep each employee accountable separately, but will also help each individual get a better sense of their group dynamics as well.

2.2 RECOGNITION AND RESPECT FROM COLLEAGUES

Employee recognition is the timely, formal or informal acknowledgement of an individual's effort, behavior or work result that supports the company goals and values and which is beyond normal expectations. Appreciation is desired by everyone, as it is a fundamental human need. People respond strongly to recognition of their work contribution, because it confirms their performance is appreciated and valued. And when they and their work are valued, their satisfaction and productivity increase, and they are motivated to achieve higher results. But achieving great results and being respected for them are not always mutually inclusive. Respect from colleagues is one of the most important incentives a person can receive in the pursuit of a successful career. It certainly doesn't come easy and requires consistent effort, but at the end the benefits are worth the sweat and tears. Earning it is just as much about diplomacy and navigating the politics of the workplace, as it is about effort.

Gaining respect and recognition is both a performance and communication outcome. Recognizing employees for their good performance relays a potent message to the recipients, their colleagues and the entire team through the formal communication channels, or grapevine. Recognition among the team members is therefore a powerful motivational technique, although it is still undervalued by management.

Problem:

A friend of mine, owning a company in the internet booking business called me complaining that he had received several resignations in only one week from employees. The reason for leaving was because they didn't feel appreciated by their colleagues and team managers, and their work efforts hadn't been valued. After speaking personally with other employees, I realized that recognition in the company was really low, which has been demotivating the staff and affecting the teamwork for a long time. It was only a matter of time before the first one leaving would trigger mass resignations.

Solution:

If employee recognition also hasn't been a core public relations activity in your company, maybe it is time to change this. In the beginning, the HR manager and team leader could start doing it discreetly, and just observe the results. A highly effective technique is to start praising people spontaneously. In stressful, challenging or even in normal work situations, many people would prefer to receive sincere thanks from those they respect at work, rather than something tangible. Whether employee recognition is given through written, electronic, personal or public praise, it should be expressed in a timely and sincere way. Here are some ideas that will help you in this case:

Tip 5: Make sure all employees receive a small daily recognition from the team leader and that the rest of the team notices it.

Establishing a daily recognition policy is an important strategy which will bring to team management the benefit of a quick and powerful reinforcement of desired employee behavior. Besides, it will provide an example to other team members of desired behavior that aligns with the company goals. When the team leader correctly applies this motivational strategy, it will give the employees at all levels the opportunity to recognize the good work of their peers, as well as their own opportunity to be recognized for their good performance.

Tip 6: Follow a 5-step process to deliver employee recognition.

Teach all team leaders in your organization to follow this simple formula when acknowledging their followers for their achievements:

- Thank the employees using their names.

- Specifically declare for what they are being recognized. In order to bring reinforcement and identification of desired behavior, the achievement should be something specific.

- Mention how their achievement made you feel (e.g. the company, the team or you personally are proud of, or respect their accomplishment).

- Indicate the added value to the company or the team by their achievement.

- Again, thank the employee by name for his or her contribution. And don't forget to be honest.

Tip 7: Organize award ceremonies at the workplace every month or quarterly to acknowledge the top performers.

What is absolutely critical for most business companies is the way they celebrate success. Those who perform must be recognized and their behavior and achievements should become an example for the others. Render positive feedback to those responsible for the success and distinguish their work. Invite them on the dais, honour them publicly and display their names in a visible place, so that everybody will get to know about it. Give the best performers special badges for them to flaunt and do it in front of all. Such types of activities tend to give a slight advantage to the team members who work hard, perform well and act as a motor for team functioning. They may also inspire the others to perform better next time.

2.3 INTERNAL COMPETITION

If the employees are unmotivated and the manager is looking for a way to inspire their enthusiasm, he or she may consider creating some *healthy competition* in the workplace. Recreational competition is perceived as fun. It often leads to increased motivation, morale, and productivity. Comparative competition to find or choose the best action, product or service is useful. It helps mobilize the team to achieve more than it would usually have, because pride and ambition discourage members from performing poorly in the eyes of their colleagues. When the given opponent is a rival company, the entire team will respond with greater mobilization and effectiveness, accompanied by lower costs and recognition demands. However, before embarking on a competition between the employees from one team, the managers should be aware of all possible consequences. Competition between a relatively small number of team members may cause hard feelings and worsen relations, resulting in reduced motivation and performance. Whether your company has 20 employees or 20,000, encouraging ruthless competition preventing the team from sharing and collaboration usually will prove counterproductive. Therefore, always consider the following negative aspects of internal competition:

- If the workers do not see a chance to win or at least to achieve a good outcome, they become discouraged. When they realize defeat is inevitable, their motivation is gone.

- Collaborating abilities and knowledge among competitors resulting in even greater performance is unlikely.

- The team may have one winner, but this leaves the rest as losers, focusing their time and emotions on that loss.

- Competition may cause resentment and feelings of revenge that continue long after the competition has ended.

In conclusion, too much internal competition is a problem. It tends to undercut trust and may become one of the most prevalent and potent barriers to organizational development, as people within the team see each other as enemies. Besides, it complicates collaboration, as collaboration means sharing. So, strong competition among those who work toward a common goal may not be wise. The motivation for teamwork and collaboration must be intrinsic and not rely on comparisons.

Problem:

The latest team functioning survey in one of my clients indicated that more than half of the sales team had lost motivation to pursue reaching their sales quota due to severe internal competition. It is a standard practice for many businesses to use the internal competition approach as a prime method to hit top targets in their sales and manufacturing sectors. Nevertheless, there are borders that shouldn't be crossed. Though it has brought him some benefits in the past, my client realized that their constant attempts to improve outcomes at any cost resulted in employee competition at that point, becoming too intense and dysfunctional, and had started threatening the overall organizational excellence.

Solution 1: *Change the standard.*

First of all, the employees should be taught to work as a team, instead of working alone in severe competition with their colleagues. The company management need to realize that when they empower sharing within the team, they support a better exchange of ideas and thoughts, and a higher chance for the unit to come to a unique idea that would be of great importance not only for the team, but also for the whole company. The team manager should be held responsible for balancing the internal competition level and introducing new standards, which aim to motivate the employees to help each other and treat their peers as a part of one big organizational family. The personal example of their superiors here is very important.

Solution 2: *Modify the competition.*

If changing the standard is going to cost you unaffordable lost profits, instead of taking rigid and costly actions against the internal competition, you may harness it by modifying it. Create teams to compete against each other. Introduce a goal that every team can win, and let the competition between the teams shift the internal team competition. Display a whiteboard in a prominent place and on a daily basis announce the contribution of each team. When the teams see their numbers going up together with the numbers of their competitors, they will continue working hard towards the required target. Ask each team to create its own inspirational motto, which has to visualize their motivation to reach the ultimate goal. Make sure the teams are selected properly and the genders are equally represented. The most important and difficult part of this approach is to decide what should be the prize. Usually, each competition has one winner and one or several losers. You must change this and make all team members winners. In order to do this, you may offer a small prize to everyone who participated and worked hard during the competition. Examples for comfort prizes are gift cards, concert tickets, shopping and restaurant vouchers, cinema and library subscriptions, etc. If you skip giving at least a small prize to all participants, you risk facing another loss in productivity shortly afterwards. The bigger prize, however, should be given to the winning team. For example, you may offer to each of them a week in a spa hotel, round trip flight tickets, or vacation in some far-off, exotic destinations.

2.4 COLLEAGUES' PERSONALITIES

Have you heard this expression: *You may choose your friends, but not your family - and you can choose your job, but not the people you work with.* It is very true! In every company there are people who constantly complain and disturb others. But there are also people who are always nice and able to improve the mood of the others when they are having a bad day. These people are very important for teamwork, as they are capable of boosting the team spirit when the team is in crisis, sustains losses, or is falling apart. Positive characteristics are easily noticed, but the bad ones aren't always obvious. There are a great number of bad habits team members can have. According to the primary research of Samantha Dillinger (2018) from Ranker voting platform, the top ten employee flaws of all time are:

1. *Lazy*
2. *Uncooperative*
3. *Takes credit for other people's work*
4. *Rude*
5. *Can't (or Won't) Follow Directions*
6. *Vindictive*
7. *Entitled*
8. *Chronic Absenteeism*
9. *Argumentative*
10. *Drama Magnet*

Not all of the bad employee traits are equally problematic, but all lead to demotivation. And as you may know, demotivation is contagious - even one demotivated employee, whose lack of interest is constant and obvious is enough to quickly demotivate the others too. Business teams are prone to the dangers of demotivated employees at all times. To tackle effectively these bad personalities in the team, the leader should firstly identify the reason behind their bad attitude. If he or another colleague can help motivate such employees, this could boost their morale and transform them into a desired team asset.

Problem:

Here is a real case scenario: You are an HR manager in a large fast food company that has outlets in different cities. You have received serious complaints from employees from different locations that some of their colleagues are demonstrating negativism, dishonesty, uncooperativeness and disorganization. You know these traits hinder teamwork, aggravate work atmosphere and worsen team spirit. In the end, productivity decreases. Do you think you have to take general actions and what would they be?

Solution: *Plan And Create A Positive Work Atmosphere Policy*

For every negative and lazy employee, there are other employees who are positive and hardworking. No manager can afford sacrificing the time and efforts of these employees and risk their productivity. Therefore, situations like this require a superior's actions. If your company doesn't have a *Positive Work Atmosphere Policy* yet, you need to call for its planning, writing, distribution and establishment among all teams. It will help your organization cope with that sensitive matter once and for all. Here are some examples of important points that can be included in the policy:

Tip 8: Communicate your culture.

Remind the team your mission statement, code of conduct, and other policies that focus on your company's values and culture. Draw employees' attention to all consequences of behaving inappropriately and violating organizational policies and existing laws. Everyone should be restrained from negativity. Instead, they have to be encouraged not to make big issues out of small ones and not to discuss their personal tensions at work. They should be taught the importance of working together as a team and what healthy relationships at the workplace mean. We are all humans, and most people react well to positive appeals that say "you matter". Nobody must forget their reason for being hired by your organization.

Tip 9: Foster a good work-life balance.

Many problems between people within one team arise when they cannot maintain a normal balance between work and personal life. Some managers are happy to see their employees putting in more than 11-12 hour days, though they know it can drain their energy and damage their health, as well as adversely affect work relationships. However, achieving a good work-life balance is important. When people fulfil their various needs and plans in their personal life, they usually feel more confident at work and become the best employees possible. Company policy ensuring a good work-life balance will foster the employees to have more real life experiences out of work, which can in turn create happiness and peace in the workplace. It will also stimulate them in developing their forward thinking and creativity, and demonstrate their positive character.

Tip 10: Encourage the employees to be open and honest.

If their working relationships worsen due to some personality traits of the team members, the first thing they should be taught is to try to honestly express how they are feeling. They have to open a dialogue. Otherwise the persons concerned may simply assume that nothing is wrong. Improving communication will ensure that the team can cope with problems before they become too serious. Moreover, they need to show some tact and respect. They are as important as honesty. It's easier to tell the truth without thinking how the others will react. But some people are more sensitive than others and direct criticism and will only make them hostile. Mistakes should be discussed carefully and then utilized as a learning experience. Therefore, the role of the team manager here is very important. It's his obligation to enthuse them to engage in productive dialogue, rather than be defensive and critical.

Tip 11: Explain to the employees why they must work closely even with persons they don't like.

It is a serious problem when some members do not get on with their colleagues with whom they are appointed to work closely. They may find them too selfish, over-confident, extra cautious, trying to take a lead, avoiding unpleasant work, or waiting until they are instructed before making any efforts. Therefore, the team manager should address this problem with patience and understanding. As people work easier with those who have similar work attitudes, he should clarify if the employees who are appointed to work closely together have been chosen properly. If necessary, he may change or shift some of them in the project to lower the internal tension. When this is not possible, he needs to explain to them that there is an important reason why they are paired with someone with a different personality. They should realize that they both have irreplaceable roles in the project and that their work alliance will bring balance and importantly contribute to the results. Besides, personality difference often kindles an excellent working relationship.

Tip 12: Ensure balance and fairness.

It is proven that many disagreements are not about differences in opinions related to work problems, but rather about balancing the work, sharing it fairly, and ensuring that credits are apportioned correctly. It is crucial that the recognition is based on the actual work that everyone accomplishes. Teach the team to be honest about their personal involvement. The team manager may keep a record of the amount of time the team members spend on a project and their contribution to the outcome. A proper respect must also be given to those who provide innovative ideas.

3. ORGANIZATION

Increased personal motivation impacting employee productivity is an essential tool for efficient team functioning that can guarantee the success of any company in the long run. Finding the factors that influence this attribute of organizational success is critical for management, as they highlight the evolution and achievement of the company. Some of them are proven to be directly related to employee motivation and organizational effectiveness. Other factors exert their influence in an indirect way. If they all correspond well to the purpose and needs of the team, employee motivation will increase, leading to optimized teamwork and higher productivity. Let's see how each of these sets of organization's factors affect motivation in their own specific way. They are classified in the following groups: *promotion opportunities, job security, trainings and team-buildings, working conditions, workload, instructions and targets, decision-making rights, and work time flexibility.*

3.1 PROMOTION OPPORTUNITIES

As promotion means deepening and growing through one's career, the lack of promotion for a long time is taken as an absence of achievements and recognition, and leads to stagnation, demotivation or even failure. On the other hand, career growth is connected with higher productivity and effectiveness, as well as stronger enthusiasm and ambition. The hope of a better future position and more power motivates many employees to dedicate their energy, time, sweat and tears in constant pursuit of company goals and objectives. There is a saying that only a growing person is seen as successful. Success, than, is not only a matter of achievement, but a process of continuous development, leading the individual beyond the expected results. Nowadays, people prefer to apply for a job that has promotional prospects and can lead them to higher positions and more power in the company. It is a fact, that promotion opportunities contribute more to employee motivation than better perks and rewards. Even experienced employees, who are in higher positions in their company can easily lose their zeal and aspiration when they realize that there are no further opportunities for career growth. The most sensitive and dangerous part in the promotion policy of any business or non-business organization is when promotion is given to an incompetent employee or a nepotist instead of other employees who are more eligible and better fit the position. Such practice leads to demoralization and disappointment among the other employees and a performance downturn becomes inevitable. Therefore, only transparent and effective procedures for assigning incumbents who have the requisite respect and credibility required of the promoted post, will benefit the company and the individual.

Problem:

The annual HR survey at an airport managing company revealed that a considerable number of employees openly aired their grievances about the lack of growth opportunities. That discontent was confirmed by the company's complaints book where other employees also indicated the problem. The previous year, management had changed the promotion policy, tightening the conditions that usually led to such. As a consequence, employees started feeling resentful, undervalued and used. Some of them contacted the labor syndicate and the issue became really unpleasant for both sides.

Solution:

You can meet similar problems in many companies, regardless of their size and growth. Usually, the issue is typical for small markets where company expansion is gradual over decades and where staff numbers vary very little. Nowadays, this problem should be approached with caution from the beginning. Besides, it is indirectly related to company's vision and development planning. However, to decrease the lack of perception of growth opportunities and effectively encourage the employees to work harder, management can use the approaches of Lazear (2000) who in this case provides the best solutions:

Solution 1: *Fair, but not overly generous chance of promotion and a reasonable pay rise.*

Solution 2: *Lower chance of promotion and a much larger pay rise.*

The higher level jobs are bountifully paid mostly not because of a higher output, but to act as a prize, encourage effort and keep the hope alive among the junior employees at the lower levels. The pay rise must not be so large that the required level of effort puts employees off and they go elsewhere, or they do not collaborate when teamwork is required and get engaged in non-productive activity.

Some great tips that support Solution 2 can be extracted from Li, Powell, and Ke's model (2018), which is contemporary, powerful and universal:

Tip 13: When the job offer itself is already pretty good, the promotion is less significant.

It means that the salaries of the entry-level employees should be higher, as well as the salaries of the managers. When the initial job offer is really good, the promotion is perceived as less important, as many employees will be motivated by fear of losing the high-paying job. This is a policy that enables the companies to keep their employees motivated even when there are not plentiful promotions to hand out. The higher payment keeps them working hard and hoping to move up.

Tip 14: If you can't offer your best employees higher salaries, instead of promotion opportunities, offer them other perks, like stock options or shares, and make them feel as your associates. Due to this, wages can stay relatively low and they, as your present associates, can reasonably assume they will become future partners, and get the benefits that come with that, later in their careers. This works well when the company is not growing and needs to compensate the employees for the lack of advancement opportunities in other ways. Thus, they choose to benefit the company in the long run, and not simply creating a short-term improvement to earn a bonus.

Tip 15: When the promotion opportunities in the company are scarce, create them.

Actually, create a long promotional ladder. Promotions have the strongest motivational power when the next step upward is never too far out of reach. Thus you can get the employees to work well while paying them the least. It can be cheaper for you to motivate them with career advancements, rather than with cash. Since the major reason employees value promotions is that they come with a pay increase, creating a longer promotional ladder with small differences in the salary levels will result in a financial saving. Plus, it will not be necessary to use the standard high pay jumps, which are fewer in number and often are perceived as unreachable.

3.2 JOB SECURITY

Since the 2008 financial crisis, job security has been a key element of attraction and retention for high-potential and top-performing employees of all ages, and in a wide variety of industries and roles (e.g. trade, engineering, production, food and beverage, technology, financial services, pharmaceuticals and so on). Employees who are confident with job security tend to have better productivity, while feelings of job insecurity can have a significant impact on their motivation and engagement. People who think their job is at risk and do not see their future in the company are more likely to look for work elsewhere, spread negative messages about the organization, and exert less effort in their work. The perceived risk of possible redundancy in the team may turn the members against the decisions of their team leader causing negativity and disrupting communications, which results in a diminution of the team's effectiveness. Besides, job insecurity exerts a negative effect on employees' health, leading to symptoms of stress, anxiety and reduced emotional resilience. Any of these may adversely impact their productivity and loyalty.

Company management plays a key role in creating and fostering a stable work environment, free of the burden of job insecurity. To allay this and other workplace related fears managers should initiate multiple actions, such as treating employees with respect, acting in conformance with what they say, helping teams set appropriate performance goals, removing operational obstacles and rewarding the top performers. Organizations that find ways to effectively cultivate and deliver such activities can successfully compete for employees who are seeking job security without offering unrealistic guarantees of lifetime employment.

Thus, they will reap the benefits of having a core group of highly engaged, productive and loyal employees who are committed to fight for the long-term success of their employer.

Problem:

Another widespread case: The stagnation in your business sector at the moment is perceived by your employees as resulting in the possibility of being terminated from service. Some of them have already started speaking about redundancy and leaving the company before being dismissed. You know there is a problem, but not how serious it is. As you cannot afford losing your best employees, what measures will you undertake?

Solution:

Your employees are feeling job insecurity! They need reassurance from the management that the company strongly needs their services, especially in periods of economic hardship. Showing them that you value their employment with your organization will help them to realize your desire to keep them and continue relying on their quality and useful work. Here are some ideas how to make the team feel more secure in their jobs:

Tip 16: Organize employee feedback activities.

If you want to break the ice and see how bad the situation is, empower the team to speak freely. Conduct an employee survey or other feedback activities, which will not only encourage the employees to share their fears, but will also make them feel valued and wanted.

Tip 17: Raise the bar for your most important employees.

Delegate more responsibility to them and engage them to work on a special project. By showing them that you trust their skills, they will feel more valued, and that their future in your company is secured.

Tip 18: Include the employees in goal planning.
Discuss with them the future timeline of tasks for their team and for each employee personally. Present specific projects and tangible objectives to give them a sense of the organization's stability and growth. Everybody should feel their jobs are secured and that you will definitely need them in the future.

Tip 19: Delegate them some small freedom to oversee parts of the work process or project in order to make them feel important. Ask for updates throughout the project, schedule them in advance, so that they may feel engaged, and reassure them that you are available if they need anything.

Tip 20: Remain busy.
Foster a secure work atmosphere and make the employees feel as the work will never end, so that their contribution will always be required. Remain busy and work as normal, assuring the team that you will keep them busy as well.

Tip 21: Encourage honest communication between the team and senior managers.
Keep the lines of communication open and let them know that if they have any concerns about their job, they are free to come and talk to you.

Tip 22: Show your employees you care about their personal lives.
Communicate with them about their hobbies and outside interests. If an employee enjoys playing football, you should keep up to date on his upcoming matches. Leaders, showing interest in the life of their followers outside of the workplace instill tranquility, and manifest confidence and commitment that the com-

pany wants to keep them as a part of the team.

Tip 23: Make the workplace an enjoyable place.
Arrange some happy moments for your employees in whatever way you can. A workplace where fun, laughter and a social atmosphere is encouraged will help you boost their morale and commitment. You can celebrate an employee's birthday or anniversary with your company. Promoting positive attitudes and discouraging negative ones will cost you nothing. When employees are happy at work, they cope easier with job insecurity. To remain engaged and productive they need to enjoy coming to work.

Tip 24: Make sure the team leaders are:

- *proactively communicative* and do not hide behind a door or let rumors circulate. If there is bad news, they should tell the truth, seek feedback and follow this up openly and properly.

- *taking care of their followers* – when people have concerns or questions, they should feel they have ample opportunity to face the team leader and freely voice their fears.

- *consistent and set expectations*, as well as to know how to reward and motivate people. Inconsistency, spontaneity and stinginess do not encourage feelings of fairness and security.

- *tolerating positive and correct relations* within the team. Expressing frustrations are important, but the team leaders must not let such fears dominate the team. This can spread negativity and reduce morale. They can initiate an open discussion, but should keep the focus on what the team can do to move forward and avoid the problems.

3.3 TRAININGS AND TEAM-BUILDINGS

Professional trainings are mechanisms that aim to cover the need of sharing experience and knowledge among the company in order to boost employee's productivity and effectiveness in short time. Team-buildings, on the other hand, are defined as a cooperative process of strong interactions within a team for increasing the energy and intelligence of employees, enhancing trust and communication, and providing specific teamwork abilities for reaching a business outcome more effectively and efficiently. As business tasks today have an increasing size and complexity, team activities often produce outcomes far below the expectations of management. Therefore, for companies which do not tolerate such inefficiencies, trainings and team-buildings are no longer just fancy options to diversify the employees and improve their work confidence, but a requirement if, of course, they want to continue in business.

Many organizations find that their employees who work closely together perform at a higher level, completing tasks quicker, and thereby remaining both effective and efficient. Building team morale and developing professional knowledge within the organization is vital, as teamwork and competence are extremely necessary to all businesses. No matter how automated an organization may be, high productivity depends on the level of motivation and effectiveness of teamwork, so staff training is an indispensable strategy for motivating employees.

In most cases, employees feel motivated when they receive free training from their employers. Training helps them increase their job skills and desire to work together effectively, which leads to increase in productivity in the organization and contributes towards economic security. Therefore, every company must have an effective training program. This will give the employees opportunities for professional self-improvement and development to meet the challenges and requirements of their tasks and work standards. This is why professional training and team-building exercises are crucial for maintaining happy and motivated employees.

Problem:

In one of the companies that I consulted, the main reason for productivity downfall was very unusual. The team alleged that bad and insufficient trainings and team-building exercises played havoc with their work motivation and commitment! Normally, it is the opposite – plenty of training activities and still low performance. In this case, the management body was dominated by old generation managers who usually tend to pay less attention to the fact that the professional training and team-building really help in fostering better understanding, co-operation, and communication within the team and go a long way to improving important professional qualities of the employees. The latter was also an important factor that had impacted productivity indirectly.

Solution:

An experienced and tight-knit team that can work in harmony is essential for the success and growth of any business. This is where the professional training and team-building come in. Training in the workplace significantly contributes towards employee motivation and building trust among the team, thereby ensuring better productivity. Besides, they prove crucial for productivity personal qualities, such as critical thinking, multitasking skill, creativity, leadership ability, determination, resilience and so on. Now that management was aware of the survey result and the importance of training for high performance and teamwork, we suggested the following, I may say very universal, traditional and cost-effective actions and the case was successfully closed:

Tip 25: Analyze training needs, identify training options, and set clear objectives for training activities.

Also, regularly review the training outcome in order to identify further training needs. In order to assess the effectiveness of your training plans and standards use the support of the following analyses:

- *Company Analysis.* This is a general analysis of the business needs or other reasons the training is required. It analyzes the company's strategies, goals, and objectives. The important questions being answered by this analysis are what is the company overall trying to accomplish, who decided the training was needed, why this training program is seen as a solution to the problem, what the history of the company has been with regard to employee trainings, team-buildings or other management interventions?

- *Person Analysis.* Analysis that deals with potential instructors and participants involved in the training process. The important points being marked by this analysis are who will receive the training, what are their level of current knowledge on the subject, what is their learning style, and most of all who will conduct the training? Do the team members have required skills? Are there changes to procedures, policies, practices, software, or equipment that require or necessitate the training?

- *Performance Analysis.* Are the team members performing up to the required standard? If performance is below established requirements, can specific training help to increase this performance? Is there any performance gap?

- *Task Analysis.* This is an analysis of the tasks being performed, but it also includes an analysis of the job and the requirements for performance of the work. It aims to specify the main duties and ability level required. This guarantees that the training which will be developed will include relevant links to the job content.

- *Content Analysis.* Analysis of documents, procedures, and laws used on this job. This kind of analysis specifies what information or knowledge is used on the job. Is that information from documents, manuals, or regulations? It is important that the training content does not contradict the job requirements? An experienced team member can assist in defining the appropriate content as an expert in subject matter.

- *Training Suitability Analysis.* It is analysis of whether training is a desired solution. Training is only one of several solutions to most employment problems. However, they may not always be the best solution. Therefore, it is important to assess whether training will be effective as per the desired outcome.

- *Cost-Benefit Analysis.* This analysis focuses on the return on investment (ROI) of the training. Effective training leads to a return of value to the company that is greater than the initial investment to perform or administer the training.

Tip 26: Plan and conduct on-the-job professional trainings and team-buildings.

This is an approach which is applied within the daily working of the team. This is the best method if you need to train new team members and integrate them into the teamwork. It is simple and cost-effective. The employees are trained in their actual workplace and learn the job by doing it. Examples of on-the-job training methods are temporary promotions, coaching, job rotation, and so on.

Tip 27: Plan and conduct off-the-job professional trainings and team-buildings.

In this approach, training is conducted away from the workplace. These methods are costly and are effective only when large number of employees need to be trained on similar tasks, within a short time. Examples of off-the-job training methods are seminars, workshops, conferences and so on.

Tip 28: Initiate a day trip.
Recognize and reward the team when they do good work with a day trip. Encourage the employees to bring along their spouses and children. It can be a good break from the daily work-related stress that can help fellow colleagues and their managers to communicate and get to know each other better. This can be counted, in many ways, as an informal team-building out of the workplace.

Tip 29: Organize group discussions.
If you need to make a serious work-related decision and have some doubts about it, try sharing it with the team and asking the employees for their opinion on the subject. Organize a group discussion and listen to their views and suggestions. In any case, it will be senior management who has the last word, but this particular act will increase team experience, promote teamwork, enhance employee understanding and confidence, and make them feel important and valued.

3.4 WORKING CONDITIONS

One of the reasons that demotivate employees are bad working conditions. They are considered just as important a job-related factor as any other factors. Bad working conditions (i.e. general workplace dysfunction) lead to dissatisfied and demotivated employees, regardless of what other motivators are in place. In order to increase employee motivation management should be concerned with the nature of the workplace itself. Conducive work environment stimulates creativity of the employees which may lead to better methods for enhancing productivity, while bad working conditions contribute to low employee productivity. Thus, latest technologies and all modern conveniences, such as air-conditioners, coffee and water machines and so on should be provided in the offices. Offices should be well furnished and painted, neat and tidy, well lit and as quiet as possible. Necessary tools required for production or service processes should be provided as well. Smoking in the office area must be forbidden. Unlike other factors that demotivate the employees, poor working conditions are easy to detect, especially in hard times or at places where companies traditionally cannot afford luxury or new machines and technologies. Let me share with you an experience I had in dealing with this problem.

Problem:

During an audit of a furniture manufacturing company, it was obvious that the working conditions were terrible. The production workshop was dirty, plus the noise of the cutting machines was not isolated and impeded the work of the remaining staff. The uniforms of the workers were stained and greasy. The office area was too small, blackened with smoke and crowded with desks. Apparently, the company did not have a policy promoting employee convenience at the workplace. Under such working conditions, it was no wonder that no one was dying from a desire to work.

Solution:

When it was realized that the employees were demotivated, largely due to the poor working conditions, we made a list of several recommendations that usually help in cases like this. Here they are:

Tip 30: Diagnose the problems.
One of the best methods to do so, as well as to supervise the effective implementations of decisions is this issue to be raised in the regular open discussions with the team. If for any reason the senior management does not want to discuss this with the team, it can use check-lists where the employees may freely express their needs, related to the working conditions.

Tip 31: Observe personally the working places.
Factors such as occupational health and safety, ergonomics, noise level, obsolescent machinery and software, cleanness and tidiness of the office, personal working space, smoking practice, and so on, should be personally observed by senior management.

Tip 32: Let the team know you are engaged in this.
Explain to the employees that it is impossible to do everything at once, but all measures should be a part of a coherent integrated approach. The improvement of working environments and conditions requires specific and separate actions which may vary significantly in form or periodicity.

Tip 33: Be realistic.
The constant pressure of urgent work problems tends to diminish

the priority given to health, safety and ergonomics, if this priority is not constantly restated. Vigilance and sustained actions are essential for maintaining and improving the working conditions, as the best devices and solutions tend to become less effective with time (tools wear out, computers become obsolescent, vehicles require maintenance, etc.).

Tip 34: Create an effective program for improving working conditions!

If a program is to be effective, those responsible for it must have, most of all, a positive attitude to working conditions and environment. And not just a morally positive attitude - good intentions needs to be accompanied by an insight into the problems and by the ability to maintain organized actions over the long term. Introduce a special policy for improving working conditions with the following characteristics:

- It should be based on rigorous enforcement of legislation, labor regulations and collective agreements.

- It should be created after consultation between senior management and employees' representatives.

- The team unit should perceive this policy in the same way as a policy for product or service quality.

- It should have a preventive capacity.

- The improvements that can be achieved by simple common sense measures should be constantly re-emphasized.

3.5 WORKLOAD

Heavy workload is an excessive amount of quantitative workload that individuals face at their jobs. Usually, salaries in competitive labor markets compensate for some undesired working conditions, including workload. But at what cost? Not only can the excessive workload be tiring, but it often drives the employees to work for longer hours than then would really like. They spend the time they would prefer to use for the things they enjoy doing and they are working when they should really be resting. Besides, constant and intense workload leaves the employees little time to deal with any emergencies that occur suddenly. This may add feelings of being out of control, hopelessness and desperation. The stress from heavy workload may interfere with employees' physical and psychological well-being, while it also has a cost for the organization. High levels of workload are related to decreased productivity, low job satisfaction, absenteeism, organizational and interpersonal aggression, and adverse employee turnover.

Recent studies reveal that employees exposed to heavy workload usually take up to five years to quit their job. During this period they face psychological damage, caused by constantly overloaded work schedules. Furthermore, they tend to quit their jobs more if their physical health is compromised by the workload in comparison to their psychological health. Therefore, voluntary turnover is a rational employee response, which occurs after long-term exposure to intense workload. Successful workload management is vitally important for their long term productivity. Unfortunately, some managers are reluctant to admit this.

Problem:

Our survey at a trading company dealing with fast-selling products revealed an excessively high workload level. It was associated with strong employee dissatisfaction, frustration, burnout indications and even cynicism. This kind of stress had been influencing negatively both employees' psychological readiness to work and their physical performance. As the managers didn't have any time (and maybe desire) to deal with the problem, the company was facing losing about 1/3 of its employees.

Solution:

Workload was found to be a significant factor of dissatisfaction in this company. We tried to increase the workload tolerance of the staff personalizing the following actions. Three weeks later we received feedback from the company, stating that the employees have become more innovative, committed and had even taken the initiative to do additional value adding projects.

Tip 35: Assess the workload within the organization.

It's important to keep a check on the expectations and demands that are being placed upon your employees. To reiterate, if someone feels overburdened by a large and impossible workload – they can soon become disappointed, stressed and lose motivation. Equally, if an employee has a workload that is too light or not varied enough, they might quickly lose interest.

Tip 36: Survey employee complaints.

Review all complaints and decide if the problem is something that can be settled through a change in procedure or policy. Look at workloads and office procedures if the complaint involves these areas. If the employees are overwhelmed by work and feel

MAKE THEM WORK (FOR YOU)

that others do not share their burden, take a look at workload distribution. Ask the team manager to evaluate the policy on work schedules and hours if personal commitments or a long commute make it difficult for your employees to work their scheduled hours.

Tip 37: Find the best resolution.

Devise a better and more efficient workflow model that distributes the work fairly to all team members. Alter the schedule if you find that valuable employees are burdened by heavy workload. When a long commute is a problem and they do a type of work that can be done from a distance, allow them to work from home a few days monthly.

If you have done what is necessary to reduce and balance the employee workload, but yet the work doesn't end, you may teach the employees the following basic routines that will help them dealing with a light workload:

Tip 38: Make them understand the strategy of the organization, the function of the team, and the corporate culture.

They have to be reminded that their role exists for a reason and it is ultimately determined by the organizational strategy and team's function. Express the organizational strategy through the vision and the mission statement of your company. Employees should be motivated to help the organization achieve its vision. Make sure they understand and perform well tasks that are strategy driven. Tasks that add value to the team, the department or the entire organization are tasks that they should always strive to complete first.

Tip 39: Teach the team how to deal with the tasks effectively.

They all have different ways of working, different styles and times when they are most productive. When they tend to work best they would use this time to do the most important or challenging tasks. On the contrary, they should complete the easier tasks when they get tired and find it more difficult to concentrate.

Tip 40: Teach employees to think critically.

They should compile the list of their tasks with allocated deadlines, look at it critically and decide which tasks they can complete independently and for which tasks they need help. Let them separate the tasks based on deadlines, completion difficulty, stakeholders requirements and dependency, and discuss their priority with the team manager.

Tip 41: Teach them to check for resources.

They must check whether they have the team's resources, support, and the competencies or training they need in order to do the job. If something is missing, they shouldn't be afraid to ask questions and communicate with relevant people before commencing the task.

Tip 42: Teach them to share concern.

When they realize they are struggling to stay on top of their work, it may help to share their apprehension and concern with the team manager or with superior managers. Sharing their fears does not mean they say 'no' to important tasks, so they must not be afraid to interact.

Tip 43: Teach them to concentrate.

They should be inspired to focus their concentration and work as if they are a person on mission. They can create a mental box around themselves during the important tasks. Nothing should interfere with them, unless of course, there is something urgent. Anything else can wait.

Tip 44: Teach them to relax during moments of stress.

They can be encouraged to practice yoga, tai chi, qigong or other relaxing methods. Despite their potential to help in coping with work stress, these techniques are often underestimated.

3.6 INSTRUCTIONS AND TARGETS

A key leadership skill shared by all high performers is their ability to manage performance effectively by setting clear instructions and reachable targets. Any team needs directions, milestones and key performance indicators. It's important for employees to trust that they will receive support when necessary and that they are able to complete the tasks within the required timespan. This will encourage them to find new solutions to problems and take initiative to improve results. However, almost every leader has been in the position where they have given a simple instruction and were amazed to see it totally misinterpreted. Unclear instructions may result in loss of time and money, frustration, mistakes and sometimes can be even dangerous. People need to know clearly what the company wants them to do and how exactly they are supposed to do it. Inexperienced leaders assume that employees understand what's required. They don't provide time to explain what they want, and then don't hold their followers accountable for the results. The norm is to tell the team to work as hard as they can and try their best. Alas, this doesn't explain to them exactly how to reach their goals.

If you set unreachable or overly demanding targets to your employees, it will also end up being counterproductive. Unattainable targets and quotas suck motivation out of them, put them constantly under pressure and make them feel like underperformers. In some cases it leads to a high employee turnover which costs the company valuable assets such as lost employee experience, knowledge and work hours, as well as incurring the need to spend unnecessary extra funds to hire and train new team members.

One of the key functions of a leader is to achieve targets and goals through other people. And while fostering creativity is a very open strategy, setting achievable team goals is more definitive. By ensuring all team members are in the same boat from the start, with clearly defined targets, the team leader empowers everyone to know where they stand and where they need to be by a fixed date. It is therefore essential that leaders can and should set reachable targets, provide effective feedback and manage the overall performance of their teams.

People can be ready to give their best, but if they don't know how to achieve an excellent performance, or targets seem impossible, management will inadvertently kill their motivation. Pointing out specific targets, reachable goals and clear instructions for performance and behavior is not difficult. When it's done, team just needs to get regular feedback on how they are performing against the targets.

Problem:

Unclear instructions and improper task allocation are present in many companies. When they become a fact, employees tend to lose their motivation to work and productivity rapidly decreases, replaced by hostility and unaccountability in the team. During a discussion with the designated person in a shipping company, responsible for ensuring that all staff follow the procedures, we concluded that part of the instructions should be better defined, as well as some task allocations to be optimized. If you were such manager, what would you do to avoid these problems?

Solution:

As soon as you identify this problem, you can use the following advice to consider improving employees' eagerness and passion to work, which I successfully used in this case, as well as at other times in my practice:

Tip 45: Set clear and reachable goals.

You must think of a goal that will boost productivity and is attainable by all. Be specific in your targets. Set carefully the necessary time frame. Goals that you present should be S.M.A.R.T. (*Specific, Measurable, Achievable, Realistic,* and *Timed*) and even S.M.A.R.T.E.R. (plus *Evaluate,* and *Readjust*). The employees should have an unequivocal understanding of what is expected from them, and everybody should believe that they can do it.

Tip 46: Motivate with clear instructions.

Usually, employees are ready to take on assigned tasks, but they'll do them better and more willingly if they are confident in the instructions given by the team leader. One trick is to think about how instructions that seem clear to the management might be misunderstood by employees. Unfortunately, that can happen more easily than one thinks. Here are a few examples:

- *When time is important.* Asking for a task to be finished by 'Friday' or even 'the end of the day' can be risky, especially if you have 4 p.m. in mind in order to give you time to review it. To a busy employee, the end of the day could mean the usual end of his or her day, which could be anytime before midnight.

- *When standards are important.* When you say you want something 'done,' does that mean completely done or just a first draft or prototype? Does 'done right' mean absolutely error-free or 'right' enough so that the main objectives are met and work can proceed? Busy employees need to know how to use their time.

- *When format is important.* Does 'written' mean handwritten notes, a copy of an email, a rough draft, or a proofread copy? Employees might think they can turn in whatever is ready by the time the deadline comes. You'll get what you ask for, so ask for what you need.

Tip 47: Train the team manager.

If the team delays with the results, or even worse - they are bad, one of the general reasons for this might be the way the team manager gives instructions. After you assess this and find out that this is the case, you can organize training activity, where this particular manger, as well as other team managers, will develop abilities to deliver punctual and well-designed instructions. Begin the training by introducing them to the three types of instructions – *orders, requests and indications*. Invite the participants to consider the characteristics of each of these types and to practice formulating instructions for a range of given situations. Incorporate practicing giving verbal instructions in exercises, like the one called 'Candle in the wind'. In this exercise they give you instructions which you follow exactly. Their objective is to get you to light a candle with a match, but they have to assume that you have never done this before. In another exercise, you divide the participants into two or three groups and ask them to prepare a set of written instructions for a given task. Once prepared, the instructions are passed over to another group for them to follow, to see if they can complete the task by following the instructions alone.

Tip 48: Link the employees to a general every day business situation.

An important factor that team members need is a clear understanding of how they fit into the big picture (business strategy, projects, market, customers, company, employees, etc.). When people don't know what's happening on the larger scene, they tend to think the worst. Successful managers are honest, reachable and open, and advise their employees about the company's vision, changes or adjustments required for the future success. They tell sincerely when business is good or bad, the future is positive or negative, productivity is acceptable or not, people are doing a good job or not. Each progressive-minded organizational management should hold at least two meetings annually plus the usual monthly department and project meetings where current situations are discussed and open to employee questions.

Tip 49: Provide incentives to reach the goals.
It shouldn't be all work and no play. Set attainable goals and provide necessary incentives for the team to reach them. They could be anything such as a lunch paid for by company, a half day off, movie vouchers, gift certificates, etc. Most important is that the team works together to reach their mutual goals. The prize at the end unifies employees, boosts their morale and eagerness to grow. Thus, your people will be more willing to understand the goals and remain focused on searching for the approaches to achieve them.

Tip 50: Include teamwork in performance appraisals.
As we mentioned before, this is a good way to improve employee collaborations and have the team members working together on important tasks. When they are advised that teamwork is included in their performance appraisals, they will know their cohesion and collaboration is being monitored and appraised. By setting clear teamwork standards you will help employees to understand their responsibilities and revive their solidarity, cooperation and trust.

Tip 51: Avoid setting common goals for all team members.
I wouldn't recommend the approach in which you take the monthly target and split it equally among all team members. It is a bad technique, as people have different capabilities and work capacity. If you incorporate it, you risk giving easy targets to high achievers, which will definitely fail to motivate them, and creating another problem by assigning less experienced or new employees unachievable targets. Every team member has to be assigned a manageable target which they can attain. This is the

best way to motivate different employees who work hard, but have different productivity abilities.

3.7 DECISION-MAKING RIGHTS

For business companies, the benefits of empowering their employees with means, time and ways to come up with new ideas are quite significant and wide ranging. One of them is the increased productivity and profit resulting from improved decision-making rights, and, related to this, the positive affect on the intrinsic motivation of employees. According to many contemporary theories, a formal hierarchy leaves the superiors unable to utilize all of their resources. In order to be more efficient in their management, often they have to lose the hierarchy and incorporate lateral communication. Such an approach equalizes the positions and encourages employees to solve problems and coordinate decisions within their team. This freedom to make suggestions and communicate with everyone leads to higher autonomy and improved decision-making abilities.

One of the greatest obstacles for delegation is micromanagement – the silent killer of motivation. It disempowers employees, suppresses creativity and innovation, and results in poor performance. Micromanagement is a guarantee that team will not reach its full potential. Instead, it means loss of control and trust, overstressed and dependent employees, lack of autonomy, high employee turnover and burnout of the micromanagers. It is important, therefore, to mention clearly that when employees are involved in goal-setting and especially in the decision-making process of the company, they are more committed towards the achievement of the goals. However, many managers would rather do everything themselves than ask someone else to make decisions on any tasks - either for fear of being too demanding or because they reckon the work will not be done well. These managers need to remember that management is all about accepting new and better ideas, as well as successfully communicating requirements and expectations, while delivering knowledge and playing a mentor role throughout the entire work process. Managers neither can nor should personally accomplish every task. They must rely on other people to achieve the company objectives. Like it or not, learning to delegate decision-making is a necessary part of each and every business management. Therefore, it is important to create an environment of empowerment and accountability in the team.

Problem:

In most of the organizations I have worked with, there were team members who considered that their decision-making rights related to the work process were limited. They clearly stated that participating only in the execution phase of the decision is the reason for the loss of their motivation and productivity.

Solution:

After studying many, and mostly complicated motivational cases, I found that different employees and even whole teams with different purposes and from different business sectors suffer regularly from limited decision-making rights or not having them at all. It wasn't the employee's position, the type of work or the purpose of the team which required these restrictions. It was the managers not willing to relinquish their power, which was at the core of the issue. Therefore, I always advise managers to reconsider the decision-making policy and practice for their teams using the principles outlined below:

Tip 52: Assess your decision-making infrastructure.

Since it is not safe to delegate before you are aware of that, the first step is to assess and if necessary create a proper decision-making infrastructure. It contains the following three requirements:

- **Right people**: Delegation is never a safe process until you have the right people to whom to delegate. When you realize you have them by your side, there's nothing to wait for.

- **Accurate performance measurement**: Delegation is a process that can be wisely monitored. You just need to establish clear metric system, which will tell you how tasks are going in real time.

- **Delegation policy**: Delegation is never a simple, linear transaction between leaders and followers. Create a policy explaining how you want the task done in your absence.

Tip 53: Decide which decisions to delegate.

The next step after establishing a decision-making infrastructure is to decide which decisions could be delegated. Effective managers decide carefully which decisions to delegate, which decisions should be discussed within the team and which they should make on their own. Ask yourself which talents, abilities and even desires your employees have for completing certain tasks. Successful managers seek where to deliver their trust and how to develop the capabilities of their subordinates. The saved time should be used for accomplishing tasks which best utilize your own strengths. Also, when you decide to assign a task to someone, think how you will manage the accountability, so that you don't lose control after delegation.

Tip 54: Empower the right employees.

Find those employees who can take the best decisions. Teach and model them how to participate in decision-making activities. This will enhance the range of solutions and effectiveness of the decisions. Besides, empowering them to utilize their practical knowledge and commensurate skills in making decisions will boost their intrinsic motivation.

Tip 55: Delegate clearly the decisions you want done.

Explain clearly what the employees are expected to do and when to have it done by. Provide them with the necessary levels of independence and autonomy to work on the decision. Make sure they know you are available for any questions, suggestions or concerns about project. Avoid micromanagement at any cost. It will only impact employee performance and make them feel that you don't trust their decision-making abilities.

Tip 56: Learn to accept failures.

Failures play a significant role in employees' growth, especially when you delegate decisions and allow them to make mistakes so as to learn from them. It's important to show your confidence in the employees. So, although the first decision was mistaken, if possible, delegate another task after the first one to manifest trust and regain their self-confidence. Delegating different tasks to your employees will make them feel more appreciated and valued among the others, and even as if they are your partners in the decision-making process. Such delegation results in greater productivity and employee motivation, and can improves the interrelations with your personnel.

Tip 57: Teach the employees the method of self-regulation in decision-making.

In essence, this process is broad enough to cover a wide variety of situations and includes three steps before making the decision - generation, evaluation and, finally, learning. *Generation* is the part where employees set their goals and generate different options to achieve them. Setting correct goals is as important as making a correct decision, because without goals, decision-making would be a response rather than a choice. *Evaluation* refers to comparing all options and assessing how probable and needed is each of the outcomes. In this phase, the best option is found and the decision is taken. The final part is the *learning* phase where employees focus on the consequence of action. It concerns the time after the decision has been made.

This model described first by James Byrnes (1998), is based on three key concepts: metacognition, motivation, and behavior. An experienced decision-maker incorporates metacognition (the ability to monitor and direct their thinking processes) in order to evaluate all options and utilize knowledge from previous decisions. People who are motivated are more likely to be confident in their decision-making abilities. Further, when they have the right behavior to use different strategies and develop comprehension during the process of decision-making, they learn to manage their impulse to take quick decisions. The model suggests that though many people don't pay attention to each of the phases, all decisions are made in this way, regardless of the speed of the conclusion. Therefore, through mastering the self-regulation process in decision-making, employees will boost their intrinsic motivation and build a stronger sense of self-identity.

Tip 58: Follow a four-step model to ensure your employees perform well independently:

<u>*Step 1:*</u> *Employees provide recommendations.* There are varieties of situations, where employees come up with problems to which you need to find solutions. Therefore, in order to make them more autonomous and independent when they need to take decisions, insist on them to recommend a solution anytime they approach you with a problem. Instead of telling them the best solution right from the beginning, take your time to ask some guiding questions and show them different perspectives and possible conclusions on the issue. Let them reach the solution alone. Though the final word is always yours, you will have the chance to coach and mentor them.

Step 2*: Employees make decisions and inform you before their implementation.* When employees are matured enough to make decisions on their own they still need to be monitored, so that their decisions should be approved before the implementation. Even if some decisions are not effective or rational, it's better to leave them as they are, unless of course they are completely unacceptable. This will bring them precious knowledge and irreplaceable experience.

Step 3*: **Employees make decisions, implement them and you are notified after that.*** This step should be taken only when employees have been regularly observed and you know you can trust their decision-making abilities. At this stage, decisions can't be cancelled, as you are notified after their implementation. There is an associated risk of bad consequences based on a wrong decision. Therefore, when you delegate decisions at this step which may cause financial loss, it's better to put a money limit on the decision – e.g. if the decision is evaluated less than USD 2,000, it could be implemented right away. Anything above this amount will still require your approval before implementation. Thus, you minimize the financial risk if the decision is incorrect and leads to loss.

Step 4*: **Employees work completely independently and you only monitor results.*** At this step delegation reaches its highest level. Employees work completely autonomously and do not have to notify you about their actions. You only monitor their results, give further directions and ask questions based on your observations. If necessary you can temporary return to step 3, until you decide your trust is well-grounded. Nonetheless, at this step, you can also set some money limits to restrict the implementation of decisions.

3.8 WORK TIME FLEXIBILITY

It's beyond any doubt that in order to be competitive, adapt to modern technologies and respond quickly to sudden changes in market demand, in our era, companies need to innovate constantly and become more flexible. Work time flexibility, however, is not identified as an important element only in employers' quest for competitiveness. Employees also prefer non-full-time working hours and flexible working time schedules in order to suit their desired lifestyles and to balance work and family life.

Flexibility at work provides employees with an opportunity to choose where, how long and when to work. Compressing the 40 hours work week into four days, beginning and ending workdays at different times, or working on specific tasks from home are some examples of worktime flexibility. The reasons could be as simple as wanting to avoid a long commute due to heavy traffic or taking children to school. Many enterprises offer these options to retain the female employees who might consider leaving their jobs after having children. According to Forbes (Schmitt, 2009), a recent study by Georgetown University proves that employee stress from not having enough time for their children is correlated with decreased productivity and increased absenteeism. The same study found that those absences were costing some businesses about USD 1 million annually.

Career flexibility is a concept that challenges the traditional career ladder of having a continuously upward path, where employees are more likely to fall back to the beginning of their career if they decide to change it. As the modern economy often follows a variable rather than a linear progression, HRM needs to deal with assessing whether employees fit their career plan. When the latter is set on long-term basis, it is more difficult to be monitored and controlled, because some of the employees may leave at the end of their career, causing losses to the company. Therefore, many companies have mapped out special career plans to bridge the gap between employees demands and company strategy. IBM for example uses the model of Kirkpatrick-Philips to provide career development. Deloitte have established their Mass Career Customization (MCC) program, which empowers the employees to work together with their managers in customizing their personal career dynamics. Employees are allowed to leave the company for up to 5 years in pursuit of other interests, i.e. to make family and raise children, to indulge in study, sport, traveling, and so on. At Grawe and Hewlett Packard, there are shared senior managers positions, taken by two persons simultaneously who are promoted as a pair. These policies aim to retain capable employees, while allowing them to develop their talents and skills elsewhere. They, however, have to meet some challenges, such as training more people for the same positions and arranging availability of an appropriate position when the employee is ready to rejoin the company.

Problem:

In a small real estate company our survey noticed employee overload and exhaustion due to lack of work time flexibility. The brokers performed most of their view trips with clients after their work time was over, because the clients (both buyers and sellers) were available in that time window, or during the weekends and holidays. They needed a complete and systematized rescheduling plan to introduce work time flexibility, corresponding to the type of their engagements.

Solution:

Here are the basic rules I discussed with the management of the company. It was really interesting to see how a little strategic change in the working life of the organization brought excellent results, such as 3 times increased productivity, considerable earnings growth, happy, healthy and satisfied employees.

Tip 59: Reconsider team flexibility.

Even if it doesn't require this, when your business allows, you may consider offering flexible work time to your employees. This is one of the best ways to show your employees that you have trust in them. Besides, the gift of floating work time is in the top ten of the most desired work perks. Many people, whether they are specialists or not, achieve best productivity when they set their own work schedule. So, if your business needs fresh ideas, higher employee commitment, better performance, and if peer cooperation is not an issue for your team, you may consider introducing flexible hours at work. But this should be well thought out, as excessive flexibility can diminish collaboration. The balance of this process depends on what both company and employees are aiming to achieve.

Tip 60: Choose flexibility options that best serve your company interests.

Discuss openly with employees about their preferences and how flexibility will help them adjust their pace, choosing the place or time to accomplish work tasks. However, if you are the decision-maker for the company, you mustn't apply all options, but only those, which, are suitable for the current business circumstances and have the best perspectives to guarantee planned development of the company. If necessary you may consult with advisers, board members or clients about these changes. In case you have already decided delivering some more freedom to your team, try to evaluate the most appropriate flexibility models which are classified in the following three main types: *full-time, part-time* and *career flexibility*.

A/ Full-time flexible options include:

- *Flexible place (flexplace)* – opportunity to work from home, satellite offices and working on the move one or a few days a week.

- *Flexible hours (flextime)* – ability to choose the beginning and end time of the working day within core hours.

- *Compressed work weeks* – opportunity to work four longer days weekly and take the fifth day off, or working a nine day fortnight.

- *Time banks* – ability to take time off as a compensation for worked overtime.

B/ Part-time choices include:

- *Reduced work week* – working several days a week, mainly four or three days instead of the regular five days.

- *Job sharing* – two people sharing a full-time position, either by working three days weekly each with one day overlapping or they alternate one week each.

- *V-time-working* – the 'V' stands for voluntary reduced hours, with customized working to a reduced schedule for an agreed period with the chance to return to the usual work hours after the period ends (e.g. during school holidays, sport or other event, etc.).

C/ Career flexibility (flex career) enables employees to temporarily change their careers taking breaks for family or personal reasons without penalties. It may also include a gradual return from maternity, starting part-time for a short period then returning on full-time afterwards, and gradual transition into retirement such as going from full-time to part-time for an agreed period before retirement.

Tip 61: Consider the following rules when you plan to manage employees who work flexible work hours:

- *Create a clear working hours policy.* For small teams and companies flexibility can be really challenging. Overloaded and stressed employees tend to leave, especially if there is no response to their claims for hundreds of overtime hours for which there are no records. Sometimes, everyone needs a day off in order to reduce the work stress from the overtime. These kinds of situations emphasize the importance of having a clear and effective policy on work time.

- *Keep a track of the worked hours.* Clearly explain to the employees how they could track their hours. Keeping a record of worked hours will also enable you to calculate the actual hourly rate for every employee and evaluate if the task is too small or too big. The record of hours worked will also help you to understand and minimize employees work stress.

Tip 62: Follow the principles for flexible work location arrangements.

Since the reason for a flexible work arrangement is to enable employees to complete work from the most effective location and in the most effective way, you may need to consider using the following principles of flexplace arrangements in your company:

- *Maintain a high level of communication.* Encourage a two-way flow of communication between distance working team members and their managers and peers. This is very important, especially when the off-site employees work alone.

- *Maintain a high level of organization and planning.* Virtual conferences often result in disorganization and waste of time, forcing managers to deal with unplanned situations and solve problems that would not happen as often as if work were well managed.

- *Divide appropriately the workload* between the distant team members and those who work in the office, so that the whole team, regardless of their work location, is treated equally.

- *Combine the face-to-face, telephone and email communication.* Face-to-face communication is best for key management tasks focused on persuasion, motivation, team-building, inspiration, decision-making, accountability, and introducing work changes. Telephone conversations, both voice and video, are very effective for quick contact, planning, reviewing, and discussing strategies. Emails are best for sending enhanced information and specific details, as well as for confirming engagements and conversations.

- *Plan team-building exercises* between on-site and off-site employees. Invite the employees who work distantly to attend to a special meeting, particular event, lunch or other team activities. After all, face-to-face communication is irreplaceable.

- *Provide the distant working employees with training and promotion opportunities.* Career development is important for all team members, regardless of the place they work.

Tip 63: Mind this general rules when introducing flexibility on work for the first time:

- *Evaluate the financial side.* Calculate the sunk costs, additional administrative duties and time in money equivalent.

- *Assess the consequences of the physical absence of distant team members.* Try to foresee the impact of members' absence on the team or the company, on meeting market demands, as well as on the terms and conditions of employment.

- *Formulate your policy.* Make a SWOT analysis of the chosen options, and develop a written policy and procedures for implementation, monitoring and control.

- *Communicate the change.* Communicate the changes to board, clients, employees, partners, suppliers, etc.

- *Reschedule meetings, conferences and training courses* so as many employees as possible can attend.

- *Manage the work load.* The work should be correctly divided, regardless of the place and time for their accomplishment.

- *Keep on meeting customer demands.* Flexibility must not interfere with customer satisfaction and the customer loyalty policy of your company.

- *Run a pilot version for a trial period and evaluate it.* Collect the necessary reports with employee's feedback and recommendations.

- *Update program if necessary.* After the pilot has started, make modifications or changes to extend or amend the program. Notify the employees about all changes in procedures.

- *Monitor and evaluate.* Continue to evaluate the program on a regular basis. Ask both distant and office employees for their feedback. Where necessary, make some changes and adapt the plans in the best possible way.

Tip 64: Consider the issues, related to flexible work arrangements:

- What are the benefits for the employees and the company?

- What efforts, money and time it will take to achieve successful flexible arrangements?

- What impact will flextime or flexplace have on your products and services to clients?

- What problems can be expected and can you potentially deal with them?

- What training is required to ensure both managers and employees have the knowledge and skills to make flexible arrangements work?

4. SUPERIORS

People are the most important part of any business. Without them no organization can be successful and operate effectively. But people are also its greatest vulnerability. They do not work in a vacuum – in order to perform their jobs and do their obligations well they have to communicate and work with others. Employers also need to manage relationships with their employees to avoid problems, keep the business running well and growing, and motivate subordinates to perform at their best. While the ideal work environment of each employee may vary, there are some general expectations which include a relationship with their superiors based on mutual respect, open communication and free of hostile working conditions. This means that establishing a good working relationship between managers and employees is one of the most important indicators of success or failure on the job.

There is a wide range of methods by which managers can impact employee performance. They include modeling behavior, performance reviews, delegating rights, constructive feedback, and so on. These methods, however, will not be effective unless the superiors foster the motivation of their employees. Fostering motivation boosts the morale, satisfaction and productivity of each employee and, ultimately, the organizational success. However, perhaps the most significant factor for establishing successful relationship with the employees is the mutual trust. To feel valued, trusted and engaged in business, employees need to be informed of what is going on with their team or organization, what are management's plans, and how these plans may affect the future of their jobs. Contrariwise, when superiors withhold information, this can lead to mistrust of management power, arbitrariness, distortions and damage to employees' morale and motivation.

Employers can keep their employees informed of the latest company developments in many ways, such as organizing common meetings and special events, sending email announcements, developing newsletters and employee portal. As trust goes both ways, employees should also feel that their feelings, ideas, and concerns can reach their superiors. Therefore, a strong employee relationship policy is able to provide the company with a consistent and fair treatment of the employees, so they will be satisfied, committed and to loyal their organization.

4.1 RELATIONSHIP WITH MANAGEMENT

Employees are like flowers, that need to be nurtured. If you give them a place in the sun, enough care and attention, and room to grow - they will be happy and will thrive. However, if you keep them in the dark, stress them too much, or neglect them, they will fail in their tasks, no matter how good they may be as professionals. Almost every company invests time and money to groom its employees to become genuine corporate assets. It will be an absolute loss for the management, if it is not able to retain its employees due to bad relationships with them. As soon as any negative issues arise, it is so important to deal with them promptly and sensitively.

If employees feel as though they are truly being valued and appreciated, they will be honest and more open with their superiors. Further, when superiors are able to get a clear picture of what is happening within their teams, it will be much easier for them to make strategic decisions and act quickly, rationally, and decisively anytime when necessary. To be really effective in building a stronger relationship with their subordinates, superiors need to understand the social-psychological idea behind important leadership actions, such as praising employees for their good work, giving them positive support without micromanaging, helping them to develop their talents and encouraging the whole team to maintain positive working relationships. Moreover, when superiors' behavior is consistent with the expectations they express, their actions reinforce the desired motivation, resulting in more satisfied, productive and dedicated employees. Motivated and happy employees stay loyal to the company for a longer period, enjoying their healthy relationship with superiors.

Problem:

Our survey in a holding company dealing with bookstore and stationery business showed a relationship gap between employees and superiors. The staff clearly stated that their managers create them problems, rather than helping them to deal with the daily work issues. These particular managers also used to order rather than listen and to escape from conflicts rather than being engaged in their management.

Solution:

These indications reveal a deteriorated relationship between the two sides. Instead of being catalysts in their organization, managers often suppress the chances for relationship development and growth. We solved this problem adequately, recommending solution based on the following rules of Cornett (2013). These advices can be used anytime when management needs to improve the relationship with employees. It's not necessary to apply all of them immediately, but if you find some particular rules are a good idea, make sure you act on them.

Tip 65: Create an open door policy.

When an employee feels comfortable coming to you with new ideas, concerns, or even with complaints, then it's naturally easier to establish mutual influence that comes with strong relationships. Try to maintain more real contact instead of webcams, emails, and instant messaging. Don't become so busy that you neglect to be accessible to your employees. Go regularly to the places where your employees do the real work of the company.

Tip 66: Set achievable goals.

No matter how smooth are relations with your employees, you will ruin them if you ask for impossible targets and impose unreasonable expectations. By following what you feel is the most egalitarian or noble route, you are actually damaging the team as a whole. Lead by example. Never ask people to do something you wouldn't do yourself.

Tip 67: Deal with any issues early.

When something breaks the psychological contract between you and your employees, you must find the problem as early as possible. Try to look beyond the conflict, reveal the nature of the problems, choose the best solution, and then implement a plan of action. Since there will always be different people to work with, the way you deal with potentially conflicting situations right from the beginning will also shape the way your employees respond to your actions and to their own work. But be aware of the importance of the authenticity of any and all information, as one of the worst situations that you, as a manager responsible for a team can get into is to get facts wrong.

Tip 68: Include the team in taking important decisions.

When team members are empowered to work together in creating policy, setting mutual goals, discussing innovations, work ideas and needs, or make other important decisions, they feel important and valued to you and your company.

Tip 69: Create an appreciative culture.

Simple words like *great*, *well done*, and *bravo*, can really work wonders and support strongly employee motivation. If someone has done his job well, do appreciate him. Encourage the others to give a pat on his back as well. Employees tend to feel pleased when sharing a warm relationship with their bosses. This step is a must in making employees devoted to your organization.

Tip 70: Do not lead only from the front.

Most managers are focused mainly on how they lead or inspire the people they are put in charge of. That is the vision of leading from the front. For some reason, the vast majority of managers feel compelled to talk about how they would lead from the front and forget to observe and listen to their teams. In many situations it is much more valuable to stand back, train and evaluate, than to task. Sometimes, we all need to go down in the mud with them.

Tip 71: Treat the employees equally.

Avoid obvious favoritism toward certain employees and openly dislike nepotism. You are not going to like them equally, but you should treat them equally. Treat your team as it is one big family and you are its parent. Enforce uniformly the rules in your organization, reward achievements the same way for everyone, and give your best to manifest a positive attitude, including to employees who are difficult to communicate with.

Tip 72: Support your employees with all possible means.

When an employee faces a personal crisis, senior management should do everything possible to help that employee and render assistance when needed. And this is not just a theory. It is something large companies typically do more often than small ones, but every company has the necessary resources and should maintain a policy of supporting its employees in tough periods. Thus, employees know their superiors will do everything they can for them during their time of need. This is also how you create loyalty and retain your employees.

Tip 73: Be sincere.

If you lie to the employees you destroy their trust, which results in a damaged relationship. Even when telling the truth is difficult or even heart-breaking, be honest – the employees may not like what you will say, but they will appreciate your sincerity. There are only three things you must never tell your employees: confidential client, stakeholder or partner information, confidential employee information, and business deals that are under confidentiality rules. Talk openly with them about your business challenges and what drives your decisions. This will show your subordinates that you don't have reasons to hide secrets from them. When you are honest and open, and embody an environment that encourages transparency, trust and support, you will be more able to achieve your goals and have an enjoyable work experience at the same time.

Tip 74: Create nice work environment.
We already mentioned that it is people who make an organization successful. The people you lead are those who interact with clients, suppliers, and partners, operate machineries or do what they need to be doing to keep the work running smoothly. Whatever rules you forced upon them, they won't make customers happy or clients feel engaged if they are not happy and engaged themselves. Nowadays, managers are somehow reluctant to give less and less of their time and energy for establishing strong relationships with their subordinates.

Tip 75: Spend quality time with your subordinates.
It's not enough only to participate at meetings and PR events. Superiors who want to have a real relationship with their employees have to be there for the good and the bad of everyday team life, show commitment to assist in the difficult projects, and share meals with the team during a rush time.

Tip 76: Be part of them.
As a manager, you are already in a position of authority. There is no need to underline that fact by treating your employees as though they are somehow inferior. Show to the team that in spite of being a manager, you don't use your status to take personal advantages or make exceptions for yourself. Otherwise, you risk provoking an *us-versus-them* response and foster your own isolation. Always show them that you are on their side.

4.2 TRUST BETWEEN MANAGERS AND SUBORDINATES

The success of any manager in motivating and inspiring subordinates is based on *trust.* When employees trust their managers, they trust their decisions as well. And even in times of uncertainty, they will be ready to rely on their superiors. The reason behind this is that they expect their superiors to do what they proclaim they are doing. However, there is also a natural, opposite relationship between managers and their employees, which comes most of all from lack of trust. On the one hand employees believe they are there to be used and exploited, but on the other hand managers consider their employees are looking to take an undeserved advantage in every possible situation. Although such perceptions are often exaggerated, the feelings of mistrust are real and aggravate vertical relationships. In most cases superiors who trust their teams and delegate decisions will achieve better results than those who are micromanaging or constantly checking for progress. By empowering their subordinates, managers are more likely to build a loyal, trustworthy and ambitious team. Therefore, the responsibility of establishing an environment of trust appertains mainly to the superiors, as they ultimately have control over the work process and are those accountable for the success or failure of the teams. It needs involvement at all levels to create a strong connection of trust and confidence in order to motivate employees to give their best in completing goals and tasks.

Actions have particularly high importance if managers aim to earn the trust of their subordinates by engaging both the employees and themselves in common tasks. Aligning words with the commensurate actions is essential for managers to build trust and ensure highly effective teamwork. When we hear people repeating what their managers promise and do, we should know that those managers have a strong impact on their perception of teamwork and leadership. But when there is a discrepancy between managers' words and actions, subordinates are reluctant to become committed and loyal to the company.

Problem:

Usually, the trust between the management body and subordinates is difficult to be identified by an external auditor. Employees tend to become naturally cautious when being asked if they trust their managers' abilities and decisions. So, even a slight doubt in their answers is a reason to assign an audit regarding the trust policy standards in the company. On one HR audit in a manufacturing company I gave the employer the opportunity to identify and address personally the current issues of the company with the simple idea to check later whether results are matching his expectations. I was surprised to hear his only answer: "My people don't have faith in me... and I don't need such people. But as I realized there are so many of them who don't trust me, I decided to call you and see where the problem is". He also said something very important, which is a typical reaction of all trust-related issues. He said they don't want to do what he asked from them. It was because mistrust always leads to disrespect. When I talked to them, I quickly realized that it was a matter of a policy, rather than a personal attitude.

Solution:

Business is all about building relationships that create trust. Managers, who don't have time to develop such relationships, lose at the end of the day. In every respect, therefore, taking time to build those relationships must become a paramount priority that would in turn make their jobs much easier. Here is what I recommend to all managers at all levels in order to build trust by aligning actions with words and impose a powerful trust policy:

Tip 77: Do what you say you will do.

Trust must not be given – it must be earned. Show your team that you live through your values, making choices and efforts that come from your conscious decision to do what you have said and promised. Use your behavior, rather than just words, to show employees that you are trustworthy and deserve their respect. Building trust is a long and difficult process, but unfortunately once earned, trust is also easily lost.

Tip 78: Show respect to your subordinates.

One of the secrets of successful leadership is to make everyone feel respected. This doesn't mean you must always respect their behavior or performance. The respect you hold for every person is based on their unique talents and personalities. It may seem difficult, but you have to find ways to show everyone that you consider them an important part of your crew. This could be a milestone in their life, especially in big organizations. Give them your time and attention, and share with them your insights and experience.

Tip 79: Be honest.

Even a single lie can waste years of building trust and rapport. Sometimes, it will be very difficult to tell the truth. Do it anyway! Don't just stick to what they want to hear. Even an omissive lie could be perceived by the employees as you don't trust them, so why should they trust you? Find out what your subordinates need to know. Communicate facts with them, but be sensitive to their feelings, open to their needs and considerate of their efforts. Maintaining an environment of honesty and openness is a necessary requisite for achieving trust amongst the team.

Tip 80: Take blame, but give credit.

If you want to lead a team, there is a simple rule: *When a team fails*

- it's manager's fault, but when it succeeds – it is a team's achievement. Practice this rule backwards and you will feel awkward and silly. A good way to give credit to your best employees is by assigning them tasks and responsibilities that will empower them and open doors to growth and success. This is a practical contrivance to make them feel like an important part of the company.

Tip 81: Be consistent.
Real trust should be built over time, not earned straight away. If someone cheats - they are most likely going to do it again. Most people naturally believe it is not something you do only occasionally. And this is how you ruin trust. The essence of your behavior, therefore, is to keep your words and commitments whatever the cost. Be a consistent person in every work-related relationship, day by day, and year after year.

Tip 82: Make employees' success your main job.
And since the essence of each employee's job is to make their manager and company more successful, employees should be convinced that you are a credible person, looking out for their best interests, and that it is a two-way process.

Tip 83: Model the desired behavior.
If you emphasize that teamwork is very important, strengthen your position by mentoring and cooperating across teams and functional groups. Try to coach, instead of merely giving commands. Leadership is more about asking the right questions than giving direct orders. No one embodies more clearly the culture and the values of an organization than a manager, who is able to influence employees' actions and drive their results by his behavior.

Tip 84: Incorporate employees' feedback.
When employees feel their voice is not heard, they may quickly

lose trust in their managers. Create a feedback system, whether it is anonymous or not, through which they can easily state their opinions anytime they want. Though you cannot incorporate every idea, make sure to acknowledge their suggestions, and leave employees with the impression that they are being heard. The best leaders are listeners and facilitators.

Tip 85: Demonstrate personal accountability.

As a manager you don't need to be perfect. Admit when you are wrong. It's hard to trust somebody who is too insecure to admit when he is wrong. Acknowledging your mistakes together with your right moves will gain your credence. Therefore, when you foster accountability, start from yourself. If employees perceive you as a normal person who is like them, they will naturally follow your lead.

Tip 86: Show your support.

Be supportive and show understanding even when mistakes are made. We are all humans, and we all need to make mistakes in order to improve our outcomes. It doesn't mean you must tolerate failure. Just don't be harsh with your team. Find balance, as blame is a trust killer. It goes a long way to build trusting relationships, but it doubles when there are feelings of guilt and blame.

Tip 87: Demonstrate appreciation.

As we said, employees need to know their work is valued. When they don't feel appreciated, they lose motivation to work hard and be committed. Being appreciative when they do great work will strengthen your relationships and support the establishment of an appreciative culture. Setting clear standards for promotions and salary raises will not only appeal to their trust, but will also encourage the whole team to gain new skills and competencies.

Tip 88: Show Genuine Care.

Employees are more than just human capital that complements the assets of your company. They have their personal lives outside the work place. Acknowledge their needs to balance work and personal time, and really get to know them. Invest yourself emotionally and let them see your care. Show them in a real human way that they can rely on your support. It will then be easier to find ways to positively reinforce them. Thus, they will become more confident in their life, more dedicated to their job, and wherever you go, they will follow you.

5. PERSONAL LIFE FACTORS

Every person has their own definition of success and this is the most important question they need to answer personally for themselves. Employees' sense of success is an important organizational issue, as it is directly correlated with their work motivation, affecting working attitudes and personal efficiency. Nevertheless, all that actually matters is their own, individual definition of success and not the organization's one. Therefore, one very strong motivational factor is personal satisfaction - how much people are satisfied with their own performance. Those who see they cannot manage with the job are more likely to lose motivation. Besides their glory and reputation in the organization due to their achievements, in most cases the perception of employees' success is also linked to some external factors, which are not directly related to their work efficiency, but have to do with their personal life. Such factors are the social status and the recognition from employee's friends and family.

An employee recognition survey held by the Society for Human Resources Management (SHRM) in 2017 showed that 73% of companies plan to make changes in their social recognition program over the next year, as their employees stated they would be much happier and would work harder, if they were recognized for their efforts by their families, friends and the society (SHRM, 2017). It's been widely proven that employees' social recognition programs can positively impact the organizational productivity, retention, and culture. Therefore, they should not be taken only as a well-intentioned initiative, but should be designed and implemented effectively, so that the employees really see and enjoy the effect of such program. However, other recent studies indicate 25% of companies do not promote or incorporate any form of social recognition as part of their HR program (Maritz Motivation, 2017). How about your company?

5.1 RECOGNITION FROM FRIENDS AND FAMILY

Despite all intrinsic motives, personal achievements are essentially meaningless without recognition and support from friends and family. But why is this recognition so important? Employees want to feel proud and valued in their personal life outside work, and for this purpose they use the power of the image of their work among society. It lets them know that their work is important and appreciated by the most important people in their life. This recognition creates more value, ascendancy and power in their personal environment. It gives employees a sense of confidence and ability to control their life. Besides, it improves their job retention. But most of all, recognition from friends and family provides a huge boost to an employee's loyalty, confidence and morale and while work achievements have their own reward, recognition from their relatives and best friends is what provides the real impetus to their motivation. Therefore, fostering such recognition is not just a nice thing to deliver to the employees. It is a management tool that rewards and reinforces the important outcomes employees create for your company.

5.2 SOCIAL STATUS

Social status is the position employees hold in society and is largely determined by their social contacts, image, and life choices. Occupation provides an example of social status that is mainly achieved, and only in some cases is ascribed. Ascribed statuses are fixed for the individuals at birth and exist in all societies. For example, a person born into a wealthy family is given many social roles as they are better socially positioned and characterized by traits such as fame, popularity, high values and talents. Achieved statuses are based on what the individual acquires during their career span as a result of their knowledge, education, capabilities, and experience. They can be achieved by gaining the right skill and knowledge to be promoted into a higher position of a job, creating employee's social identity within the occupation.

Apart from financial payoffs, social status seems to be one very important incentive and motivating force of employees' behavior. Status is also used as a token of prestige and honor when it denotes the relative position of people on a publicly recognized scale or hierarchy of social privileges and worth. As the differences between the *haves* and *have-nots* have been very conspicuous during the economic recession of recent years, people become more concerned about their status, especially when its disparities are more noticeable. Low-status employees are much more sensitive to being socially rejected, which makes them more inclined to monitor their environment for potential threats. Due to this vigilance to protect their sense of confidence and self-worth, low-status people tend to respond more quickly and violently to personal threats or insults, which inevitably interferes with the quality of their work. Therefore, maintaining high social image is used by many organizations in many parts of the world to retain and motivate employees, as well as to increase their self-confidence, career ambition and working spirit.

Problem:

In one of my latest surveys I found that almost 80% of the staff were showing signs of inertia, apathy and lack of interest to actively participate in decision-making and task-distribution. Besides, in spite of the pay-to-performance practice in the company, many of them were somewhat indifferent towards their achievements, and were not excited to discuss their potential contribution to generating innovations or suggestions to improve results. After checking all possible reasons, such as payment and benefits satisfaction, relationships with managers and peers, work conditions, workload and so on, I didn't find anything significant, that would cost 4/5 of the employees to lose their motivation and passion to work. It took me quite an effort to realize one crucial correlation that cleared the matter up. Those who were demoralized stated low recognition from their friends and family with respect to their work. Besides, they were also unhappy with the social status, provided by their job. Of course, there were other reasons as well (it was a difficult case), but that reason was the leitmotif.

Solution:

Together with the other means that the company was supposed to undertake in order to regain employee motivation, we recommended special advices, aiming to help the employees feel more valued and appreciated in their personal life. Here are the main techniques which are practical and don't cost much, but in return may strongly help in solving this unpleasant problem:

Tip 89: Organize award ceremonies and holiday parties at public places to acknowledge the top performers.
Each company needs to celebrate and learn from its successes

and motivate its employees to continue their hard work. Award ceremonies are events where that can happen. Honour your best employees in front of their families and colleagues. Manifest their names publicly and in the presence of all, so that everybody gets to know about their achievements. Give some small recognition awards to other employees as well. This will inspire them to perform better next time.

Tip 90: Present the recognition publicly, so that the relatives and friends of the employees may see or hear it. Even if people are uncomfortable with publicity, it is important for their families to feel proud of them. Social medias are the best platform for this purpose. Create a proper hashtag for your awards so that everybody can join the conversation and share pictures and excitement from the event. This will bring the winners extra glory and help raise their social status and prestige. Building excitement about your ceremony and sharing headlines on company's progress will also add value to your company.

Tip 91: Write out a recognition letter when you celebrate achievements.
Express in written form what your best employees did, why it was important for the company, and how the actions served your organizational development. Make the letters look shiny and official.

Tip 92: Write a personal note to the most important employees on their birthdays, signed by the CEO and their supervisors or team leaders. Thank them for their work efforts and promise them promotion. And of course never forget to fulfill what you have promised!

Tip 93: Provide additional cash or vouchers in their gift cards, certificates, and recognition letters. When you use a consumable form of employee recognition, accompany the cash with a letter or note. When the money has been spent, you need the employees to remember the recognition.

Tip 94: Accompany the written and verbal recognition with a gift, which can be seen or used by employees' families and friends (e.g. watch or short vacation family tickets). Even some small gifts like engraved plaques, certificates of appreciation or merchandise that carries the company logo will reinforce their recognition.

Tip 95: Assign your best employee to represent you at a meeting outside the company.

If the meeting is out of the region, offer the person to take his spouse on the business trip and cover the expenses.

5.3 PERSONAL SATISFACTION

Personal satisfaction from the job done is positive and pleasurable emotional state that results from employee self-appraisal of their job or job-related experience. Generally, it comes from the self-perception of how well employees do their job and provides those things that are viewed as important in their organization. Every member of the team has their own personal criteria about how well they manage with their job. They deal with their own standards in a very private way. Personal satisfaction, therefore, is a unique emotional response to a job situation and as such, it cannot be seen, it can only be inferred. Absence of personal satisfaction may lead to lethargy and reduced commitment, and is often a predictor of quitting a job.

Many times in my career, I have seen employees on different hierarchy levels, with different jobs and obligations having one problem in common – personal dissatisfaction of their own progress or work results. I would even name it *a personal dissatisfaction syndrome*, whose core is hidden mainly in the individuals' relationships with their families during their childhood or period of maturity. Unlike its social role, causing these young people to constantly search for better alternatives in society and in their intimate relations, which make them extremely sensitive to the need of change and exhausted in their infinite attempts to finally find what they are looking for, *personal dissatisfaction syndrome* at workplace can be something positive if managed well by leaders. Constant striving for perfection can give an impetus to higher commitment, motivation and productivity. Besides, it can be used as a leading example for other employees, whether they are experienced or newcomers. In many organizations, perfectionism is a desired trait driving an employee to set high performance standards and strive for flawlessness. When it is accompanied by critical self-evaluations and concerns regarding others' standards, those employees are able to become naturally the heart of a high-performing team every leader wants to run. The challenge is to find a way to keep them working for you and make them recognize your company goals as their own.

Problem:

During a consultation with the HR manager of a machinery production company I was engaged in doing my routine team functioning survey, in which part of the personnel indicated a lack of personal satisfaction. Some of them stated physically heavy tasks and the impossibility to shift to another part of the product cycle manufacturing, while several of the longer-tenured employees were complaining of doing monotonous jobs and lack of opportunity to participate in other technological processes that would fit them better. The management was looking for a quick solution that would put everything in order as soon as possible.

Solution:

At this juncture, the level of personal satisfaction of some workers was far below the norm for a long time. As the qualifications of those employees did not allow shifting due to job requirements and labor regulations, the HR manager determined that it would be best to offer an exit plan to some of the employees operating in a negative state, causing permanent bad feelings as a probable mechanism of social comparison. As it was questioned whether they could be realigned from a positive attitude perspective, in order to reduce the tension in the work climate, workers exhibiting negative dispositions were allowed to leave. In this case dispositional factors (workers' characteristics) were simply too difficult to overcome for some employees. So, in order to avoid circumstances requiring last minute solutions, as soon as you notice such problem within your company, you may use the following tips to raise the spirit of your employees:

Tip 96: Look Inward.

It would be pertinent to talk to those employees and try to understand what causes the dissatisfaction. Reasons for personal dissatisfaction at the workplace are really multifarious. If it is a personality issue, it's important to empathise and understand all personal driving motives. Managers are not psychologists, but the job requires them to act as if they are such. As they say, a problem shared is a problem halved.

Tip 97: Discuss opportunities in a positive manner.

Revise your company policies and practices, meet with your employees and discuss career mapping and internal job-shifting opportunities. If they are unhappy about their work achievements negotiate their deliverables and outcomes. Ask them if they need any resources. Find a way to end the discussion positively. Encouraging employees to share negativity or highlight their dissatisfaction could ultimately impinge the others and affect the quality of their output.

Tip 98: Divide bigger goals into smaller and daily goals.

Nothing cure dissatisfaction like a feeling of accomplishment. If possible, break your big team and personal goals down into smaller manageable tasks that those employees can accomplish in a day. Don't forget to check the accomplishments off in order to wake up feelings of sufficiency and completeness in their hearts. If they are genuinely struggling to prove themselves guide and monitor their exponential progress until they become able to contribute and accomplish more than they ever thought possible.

Tip 99: Increase gradually job demands and monitor the team.

Interestingly, commitment and high-quality performance are greatest and lead to personal satisfaction when the demands of the job are highest. This is a universal principle, which could be applied even to low-level jobs, such as those at manufacturing plants or fast-food restaurants. But be careful, as higher job demands should be supported by adequate recognition for the well done job, promotions, additional payment, and benefits. Besides, it is recommended mostly when currently the team members do not have clear and correct job demands. Therefore, in spite of its effectiveness, this motivational technique should be carefully planned and applied. Otherwise, there is a risk extremely high job demands to cause the opposite effect and decrease satisfaction and motivation in the team.

Tip 100: Develop supportive relationships with your employees.

You are in charge of your relationships with your subordinates. From the quality of these relationships depends how well you achieve your goals as a manager. You may have all of the information you need to succeed, but you can't accomplish your tasks all alone. So, you share a critical interdependence with your employees. This means that, in a way, you share the responsibility of their personal satisfaction with them. Apropos, they may not become satisfied and progress without your support, experience, information and knowledge. Therefore, maintain constant and effective interaction and feedback with your employees.

CONCLUSION

Motivation is essential when faced with any task in life. In terms of team functioning, motivation is the combination of individuals' energy, willingness and desire directed from all team members at achieving a common goal. It represents the cause of action and is the reason for employee commitment and passion to work. Employees who are adequately motivated to perform are more productive, dedicated and engaged in their work. Creating motivation means to make your employees want to do the things they know should be done. We all have seen people who know how to do the things correctly and have all available resources, but for one reason or another, they choose not to do so, which automatically makes it a motivational issue. Motivation-related obstacles could arrive from many directions. Many jobs have problems that are distinctive to the position. However, it is the problems distinctive to people that normally cause them to lose interest and focus of their main duties and obligations.

There are many rules to motivate employees, and most of them follow three main simple principles:

- Show them that the good work is rewarded

- Make them feel treated fairly

- Make them believe that their work is important and meaningful

The principle of expectancy outlines the connection employees expect between effort and reward. If they work very well and put forth additional efforts, they will likely expect to be rewarded accordingly. Employees who do not feel rewarded or treated equally become unmotivated. Therefore, employers need to ensure that their employees can rely on positive outcomes when they are committed and work hard all day long. When reward is not fair, working relationships and conditions are bad, or employees are treated poorly, it is unlikely that your team will produce great results. This may look like an obvious point, but it is vital to the success and longevity of your business to establish a motivational culture that guarantees not only committed and hungry for work employees, but also employees who are loyal and devoted to your organization. Meaning, you have to take care of their career motivation as well. In its core, career motivation is a set of individual characteristics that are associated with career behaviors and decisions, and determines personal career identity and resilience. It should take a decent place in your motivational culture planning.

As we said, motivational culture is strongly related to organizational success. Motivated employees increase productivity and allow the company to achieve higher levels of output, while demotivated employees lead to loss of revenue and productivity, and often cause problems with the relationship between the business and its customers. Therefore, it is important for people who are in a management role to understand well how employees are motivated, and what they can do as managers to keep them motivated. It's important to know that motivation is individual, and the degree of success achieved through one single strategy may not be the most effective way to move all employees. The most effective way to determine what triggers this feeling in others is through carefully studied motivational factors.

All teams are originally unique. Their organizational cultures and type of business make them even uniquer. My recommendations in this book were based on collective results of different teams, each having their own particulars in relation to the explained motivational factors. Although they consist of long-proven methods and techniques of employee motivation, they are not completely universal and may not be valid for all teams. Therefore, when dealing with employee motivation issues, managers must not undertake actions before getting clear what the big picture is and making sure that the chosen moves are the most proper and correct actions in the specific circumstances. For this, some managers may need to hire an additional advisor or auditor, whether they are internal or external for the organization. Thus, I believe they can receive an indispensable help in their efforts to create better and more workable atmosphere that empowers committed and happy teams.

◆ ◆ ◆

Finally, I'd love to hear your feedback on this book! Which tips and solutions do you think will be most helpful for you? I'd be happy to receive your suggestions, ideas, proposals or questions on my email below.

If you're experiencing any human resource management hardship (whether related to motivation, loyalty, leadership, team assessment, change management, etc.), write me and I promise you'll receive the care, attention, and time you deserve. I will listen to you carefully and communicate to you so we can find together the best solution for your case. You don't need to fight problems alone. Use allies!

Boris Gramchev

gramchev@marimex-bg.com

ABOUT THE AUTHOR

Boris Gramchev is an HR consultant, entrepreneur, lecturer and researcher in HRM & Leadership. He is founder & CEO of business companies Marimex, and Odessos Consulting Group – a software startup specializing in HR audit and change programs design in large, medium and small enterprises. His work explores team functioning, particularly the forms of interaction between team dynamics, selection and organizational culture. Boris is also a founder & director of the Institute of Team Functioning®, which develops the role of teamwork management in revitalizing under-performing teams in the context of modern organization. Before his research career, he was a CEO of Sea Global Holding, where he managed strategic activities in the areas of real estate, construction, manufacturing, and trade. Earlier in his career, Boris was a naval officer, ship manager, senior ISO, ISM and ISPS auditor.

In 2012 Boris was awarded the MBA STUDENT OF THE YEAR at Cardiff Metropolitan University. He is also a Master in Maritime Navigation from Bulgarian Naval Academy, in addition to BAs in International Economic Relations and International Law from Sofia's University of National and World Economy. Boris has received additional qualifications in leadership, team development and auditing at the International Business Management Institute – Berlin, ÖHMI EuroCert® - Magdeburg, European Proskills Institute, and Panama Maritime Survey & Certification Services.

BIBLIOGRAPHY

Adair, J. (2006). *Leadership and motivation: the fifty-fifty rule and the eight key principles of motivating others.* London: Kogan Page.

Byrnes, J. (1998). *The nature and development of decision-maker: A self-regulation model.* Hillsdale, NJ: Erlbaum.

Cornett, J.E. (2013). How to Build a Stronger Relationship With Your Employees. *Houston Chronicle.* n. page

Dillinger, S. (2018). The Worst Traits for an Employee, retrieved from https://www.ranker.com/list/bad-employee-characteristics/samantha-dillinger on 09.11.2018

Herzberg, F., **Mausner**, B., & **Snyderman**, B. (1959). *The Motivation to Work.* New York: John Wiley.

Hofstede, G. (2001). *Culture's consequences: comparing values, behaviors, institutions, and organization across nations* (2nd ed.). Thousand Oaks: Sage Publications.

Ke, R., **Li**, J. & **Powell**, M. (2018). Managing Careers in Organizations. *Journal of Labor Economics*, University of Chicago Press, vol. 36(1), pages 197-252.

Lazear, E.P. (2000). Performance Pay and Productivity. *American Economic Review.* 90(5), pages 1346-1361.

Maritz Motivation Solutions (2017). Employee Engagement & Recognition Benchmark Study. Retrieved from: http://go.maritzmotivation.com/benchmarks_study on 13.12.2018

Maslow, A.H. (1943). A theory of human motivation. *Psychological Review.* 50 (4), pages 370–96.

Schmitt, E. (2009, March). How A Flexible Work Schedule Can Help You Strike The Balance. Forbes. Retrieved from: https://www.forbes.com/2009/03/16/work-life-flextime-leadership-careers-flexible on 29.11.2018

Society for Human Resources Management (2017). 2017 SHRM Conference Recognition Survey Results: Onboarding, Rewards & Recognition. Retrieved from: https://www.shrm.org/hr-today/trends-and-forecasting/research-and-surveys/pages/surveysby-date.aspx on 13.12.2018

 Vroom, V. (1964). *Work and Motivation*. New York: Wiley and Sons.

www.ingramcontent.com/pod-product-compliance
Lightning Source LLC
Chambersburg PA
CBHW072149170526
45158CB00004BA/1566